Cooking is Easy

Cooking really *is* easy with this book, which tells you how to make everything from a quick snack to a full-scale meal for the whole family. There are ideas for feeding your friends, exciting treats for special occasions, recipes for baking cakes, biscuits and sweets, plus a special section about outdoor eating – cooking for picnics, barbecues and camping. All the recipes in the book have been tested in the Hamlyn Kitchen.

Useful notes at the beginning explain cooking terms, oven temperatures, kitchen tools, how to plan your cooking and – most important – safety in the kitchen. So put on your apron, roll up your sleeves, and start preparing the feast of a lifetime!

Jane Todd was the Cookery Editor of *Woman's Own* before she became Cookery Editor for the Hamlyn Group. She has written a number of successful cookery books for both children and adults.

Cooking is Easy

Jane Todd

Illustrated by Marilyn Day
Cartoons by David Mostyn

Beaver Books

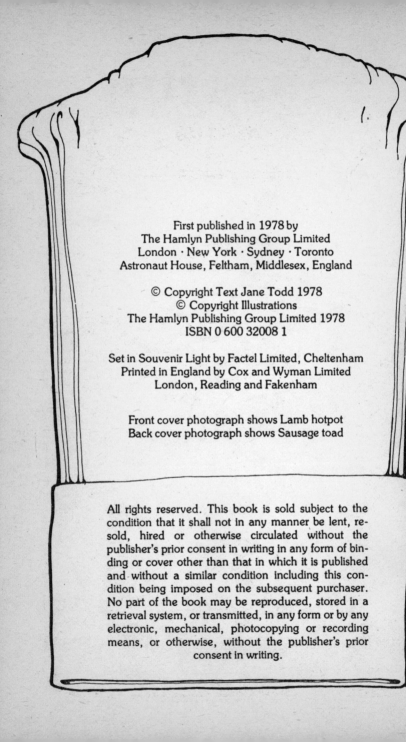

First published in 1978 by
The Hamlyn Publishing Group Limited
London · New York · Sydney · Toronto
Astronaut House, Feltham, Middlesex, England

© Copyright Text Jane Todd 1978
© Copyright Illustrations
The Hamlyn Publishing Group Limited 1978
ISBN 0 600 32008 1

Set in Souvenir Light by Factel Limited, Cheltenham
Printed in England by Cox and Wyman Limited
London, Reading and Fakenham

Front cover photograph shows Lamb hotpot
Back cover photograph shows Sausage toad

Contents

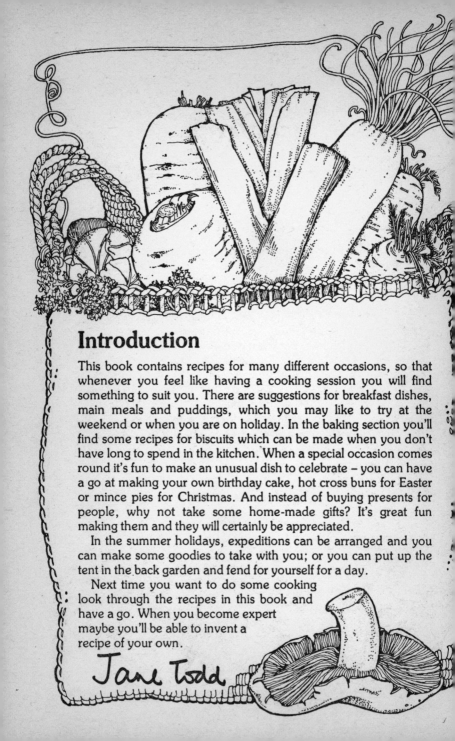

Introduction

This book contains recipes for many different occasions, so that whenever you feel like having a cooking session you will find something to suit you. There are suggestions for breakfast dishes, main meals and puddings, which you may like to try at the weekend or when you are on holiday. In the baking section you'll find some recipes for biscuits which can be made when you don't have long to spend in the kitchen. When a special occasion comes round it's fun to make an unusual dish to celebrate – you can have a go at making your own birthday cake, hot cross buns for Easter or mince pies for Christmas. And instead of buying presents for people, why not take some home-made gifts? It's great fun making them and they will certainly be appreciated.

In the summer holidays, expeditions can be arranged and you can make some goodies to take with you; or you can put up the tent in the back garden and fend for yourself for a day.

Next time you want to do some cooking look through the recipes in this book and have a go. When you become expert maybe you'll be able to invent a recipe of your own.

Jane Todd

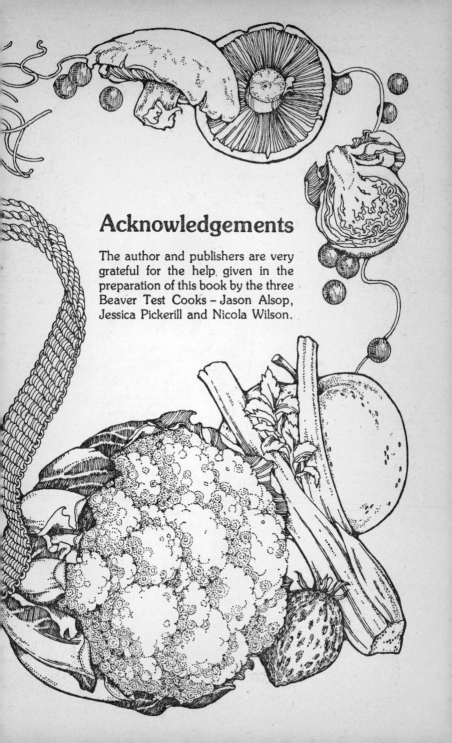

Acknowledgements

The author and publishers are very grateful for the help given in the preparation of this book by the three Beaver Test Cooks – Jason Alsop, Jessica Pickerill and Nicola Wilson.

Kitchen tools and how to use them

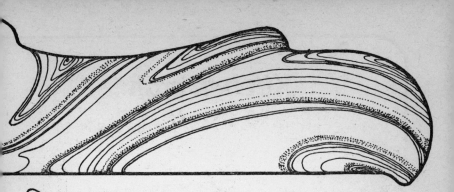

Cooking will be much easier for you if you use the right tools for the right job. Here's a list of kitchen tools explaining what they may be used for.

Wooden spoon Use for mixing ingredients together and for stirring a mixture in a pan.

Kitchen scissors Use for removing bacon rinds, snipping chives and marshmallows.

Knives Use for cutting and chopping various ingredients. Never chop or cut on the table – use a wooden board. Be very careful when you are using a knife.

Wire tray Use for cooling your cakes after they have been turned out of the tin to stop them going soggy.

Baking tray A flat tray used for baking biscuits.

Cutters Use for cutting out pastry for mince pies, biscuit dough or scones.

Pastry brush Use to dip in milk and brush over uncooked food to make it shiny when cooked.

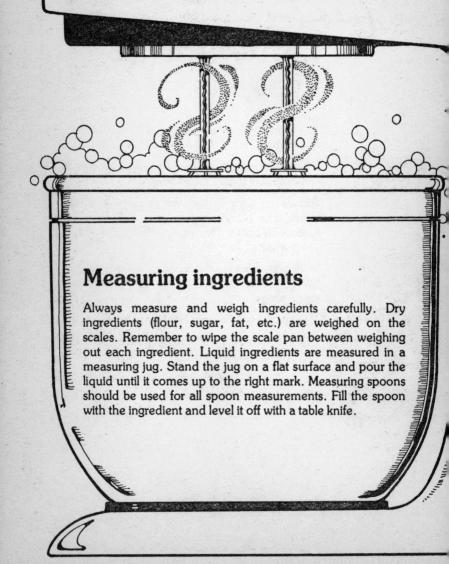

Kitchen craft

Here are a few guidelines to ensure that your cooking will be successful.

Measuring ingredients

Always measure and weigh ingredients carefully. Dry ingredients (flour, sugar, fat, etc.) are weighed on the scales. Remember to wipe the scale pan between weighing out each ingredient. Liquid ingredients are measured in a measuring jug. Stand the jug on a flat surface and pour the liquid until it comes up to the right mark. Measuring spoons should be used for all spoon measurements. Fill the spoon with the ingredient and level it off with a table knife.

Some cooking terms

To cream This means to beat two ingredients together (usually fat and sugar for cakes) with a wooden spoon until they are light and fluffy. This must be done properly to make sure that your cakes are successful. When creaming, stand the mixing bowl on a damp dish-cloth to prevent it from sliding about on the table.

To whisk This means getting air into a mixture to make it light. For whisking use a rotary or balloon whisk.

To knead This is done with your hands to make a mixture smooth. A mixture is kneaded on the table.

To rub in This means rubbing one ingredient into another with your fingertips until the mixture looks like breadcrumbs. This is done when making pastry and some other baking recipes.

To sieve This means passing an ingredient (e.g. flour) through a sieve to get rid of any lumps.

To boil This means cooking foods in a liquid which has reached a certain temperature. A liquid which is boiling has bubbles on the surface.

To simmer This is cooking in a liquid which isn't quite as hot as a boiling liquid. You should see occasional bubbles on the surface of a simmering liquid.

To fold in This is a very gentle movement done with a metal tablespoon. Flour is folded into a creamed or whisked mixture when making a cake.

Safety Rules

Before you start to make any of the recipes in this book it is very important that you read the following rules and remember them. Don't forget that the food you are cooking, the utensils you are cooking it in and the stove itself all get very hot, and it is all too easy to burn yourself.

1 Check with your Mum that it's all right for you to use the kitchen. *Never* have a cooking session when all the grown-ups are out of the house.

2 Concentrate on your cooking and don't try to do other things at the same time.

3 Keep saucepan handles turned inwards towards the cooker. If they stick out, you, or a brother, sister or friend could accidentally knock them off the cooker.

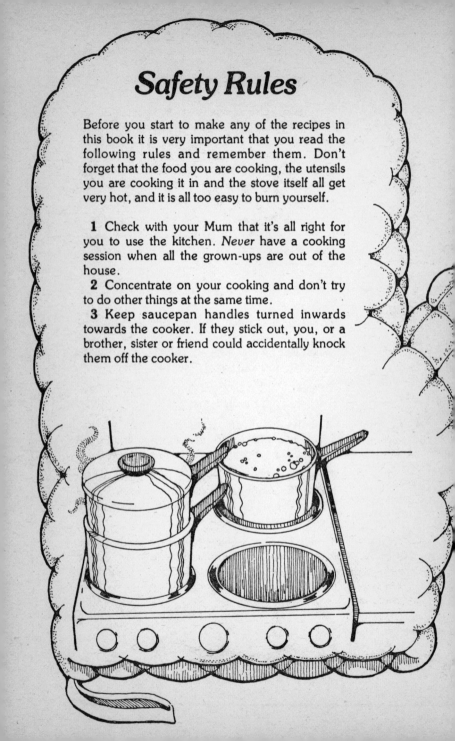

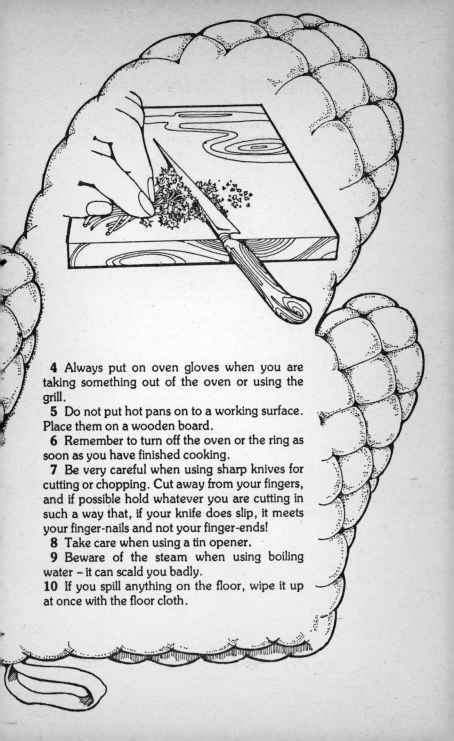

4 Always put on oven gloves when you are taking something out of the oven or using the grill.

5 Do not put hot pans on to a working surface. Place them on a wooden board.

6 Remember to turn off the oven or the ring as soon as you have finished cooking.

7 Be very careful when using sharp knives for cutting or chopping. Cut away from your fingers, and if possible hold whatever you are cutting in such a way that, if your knife does slip, it meets your finger-nails and not your finger-ends!

8 Take care when using a tin opener.

9 Beware of the steam when using boiling water – it can scald you badly.

10 If you spill anything on the floor, wipe it up at once with the floor cloth.

Planning your cooking

By now you will probably be itching to get into the kitchen and start cooking, but in order to achieve the best possible results remember:

1 Read the recipes through from the beginning so that you can check that all the ingredients and utensils are in the kitchen.

2 Collect all the ingredients and equipment you will need.

3 Follow each stage of the recipe carefully.

4 Before you start arrange the oven shelf in the correct position (where a recipe tells you to put the shelf on the second or third runner it means the second or third runner from the top), and heat the oven to the required temperature.

5 Wear an apron and wash your hands before you start.

6 Choose a recipe to fit in with your timetable. Don't decide to make a cake if in half an hour you want to go out or watch the television.

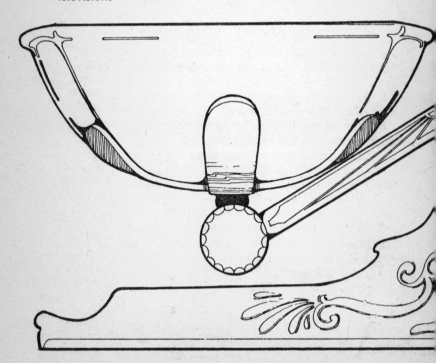

7 Remember that hot food should be served on warm plates. The plates can be put to warm either in the warming drawer, the space under the grill or in a low oven, depending on which is the most convenient.

8 All good cooks wash up as they go along and leave the kitchen tidy. To make the washing-up easier, soak dirty utensils in water as soon as you have emptied them. This prevents food from sticking to the sides.

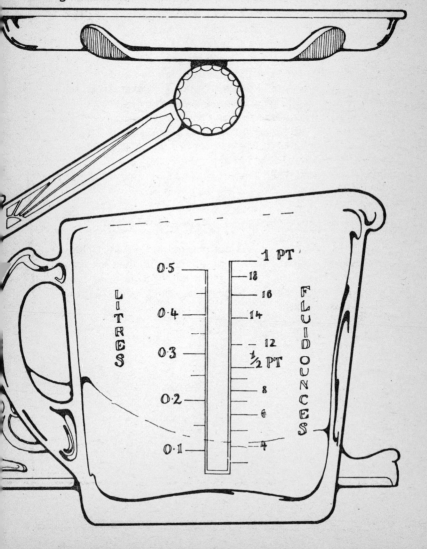

Some useful facts and figures

All the measurements are given in metric units and soon we shall be using them all the time. If you have cookery lessons at school your teacher will use metric measures so you will be familiar with them, and when shopping for your ingredients you will see that many goods – for example, flour, sugar and canned foods – are sold in metric packs. However, when you go to buy meat from the butcher and fruit and vegetables from the greengrocer, you will have to ask for the amounts you need in pounds, until a future date when our shopkeepers will weigh everything in grams and kilos. For the time being, it is helpful to know that 450g is approximately 1lb, and 1 kilogram is a little over 2lb.

Oven temperatures

New electric cookers are marked in degrees Celsius, but if your cooker at home has Fahrenheit markings this chart will guide you. In each recipe three oven markings have been given – Celsius, Fahrenheit and Gas Marks.

Oven description	°C	°F	Gas Mark
Very cool	110	225	$\frac{1}{4}$
	120	250	$\frac{1}{2}$
Cool	140	275	1
	150	300	2
Moderate	160	325	3
	180	350	4
Moderately hot	190	375	5
	200	400	6
Hot	220	425	7
	230	450	8
Very hot	240	475	9

Grams and millilitres

Dry ingredients (such as sugar, flour and fats) are measured in grams (g). Liquid ingredients are measured in millilitres (ml) and, for larger amounts, in litres. In case you don't have metric measuring scales (for the grams) and a metric measuring jug (for the millilitres and litres) here's a chart which shows the measurements to use if you are working in ounces and pints.

Metric (grams)	Imperial (lb and oz)
25g	1oz
50g	2oz
75g	3oz
100g	4oz
150g	5oz
175g	6oz
200g	7oz
225g	8oz
250g	9oz
275g	10oz
300g	11oz
350g	12oz
375g	13oz
400g	14oz
425g	15oz
450g	16oz (1lb)

Metric (millilitres and litres)	Imperial (pints)
150ml	$\frac{1}{4}$ pint
300ml	$\frac{1}{2}$ pint
450ml	$\frac{3}{4}$ pint
600ml	1 pint (20 fluid ounces)
1 litre	$1\frac{3}{4}$ pints

Notes for American and Australian users

In America the 8-oz measuring cup is used. In Australia metric measures are now used in conjunction with the standard 250-ml measuring cup. The Imperial pint, used in Britain and Australia, is 20 fl oz, while the American pint is 16 fl oz. It is important to remember that the Australian tablespoon differs from both the British and American tablespoons; the table below gives a comparison. The British standard tablespoon, which has been used throughout this book, holds 17.7 ml, the American 14.2 ml, and the Australian 20 ml. A teaspoon holds approximately 5 ml in all three countries.

British	American	Australian
1 teaspoon	1 teaspoon	1 teaspoon
1 tablespoon	1 tablespoon	1 tablespoon
2 tablespoons	3 tablespoons	2 tablespoons
3½ tablespoons	4 tablespoons	3 tablespoons
4 tablespoons	5 tablespoons	3½ tablespoons

A metric/American guide to solid and liquid measures

Solid measures

Metric	American
450g butter or margarine	2 cups
450g flour	4 cups
450g granulated or castor sugar	2 cups
450g icing sugar	3 cups
225g rice	1 cup

Liquid measures

Metric	American
142ml liquid	⅔ cup liquid
248ml	1¼ cups
568ml	2½ cups

PART 1 – INDOOR EATING

This section of the book gives lots of recipes for all types of occasions. Whether you want to cook a main meal, bake a cake, make biscuits or sweets; or produce a birthday cake for yourself or your brother or sister, the recipes are here. They are grouped into separate sections so that you can find a particular type of recipe easily. The little drawings at the top of each page show the type of recipe you will find on that page.

But before you start on your cooking adventure, make sure you have read the notes on pages 9 to 18.

Breakfast Dishes

Breakfast is the most important meal of the day and it is one which you should not miss. It isn't necessary to have a cooked breakfast every day but you shouldn't leave for school without something inside you.

Food for breakfast must be quick and easy to prepare as time is usually short. When you plan to cook the breakfast it's a good idea to do some preparation before you go to bed on the previous evening – you can set the table or get the breakfast tray ready if you plan to give Mum a treat or take her breakfast up to her.

Breakfast foods

Fruit juices These can be bought in cans, jars or frozen containers. When using the *canned juices*, open the can and pour the juice into a jug which can be stored in the refrigerator. *Jars of fruit juice* can be stored in the refrigerator and poured from the jar – remember to give the jar a shake before pouring the juice into a small glass. *Concentrated frozen juices* should be made up into a jug with water, according to the directions on the can, and stored in the refrigerator. If the juices are left standing in the refrigerator you will need to give them a stir before pouring them out so that they are well mixed.

Grapefruit This is a citrus fruit which means that it has plenty of Vitamin C – an important vitamin to have in your breakfast menu. *To prepare a grapefruit for breakfast,* cut it in half using a stainless steel knife and place each half in a sundae glass or on a small plate. With a sharp-pointed knife cut all the way round each half between the skin and the flesh and then cut between the segments. Remove the core and sprinkle the fruit with castor sugar.

Cereals Everyone has their favourite cereal and there are lots to choose from. Instead of having milk over your cereal why don't you spoon some fruit-flavoured yogurt over it?

Toast Put fairly thick slices of brown or white bread under the heated grill and brown them on each side – do not go away while the toast is browning otherwise you will have burnt toast! As each slice is ready, place it on a board, cut it in two and stand each half in a toast rack. Do not pile the hot toast up – this will make it soggy.

Another way of making toast is to use an electric toaster. This way you don't have to watch it, as the toast pops up when it is done. Simply place the bread slices in the toaster, press the lever down and wait for the toast to pop up.

Creamy porridge

To make a really creamy porridge, leave the rolled oats and water to soak in the pan overnight.

Serves 4

Ingredients
75g rolled oats
600ml cold water
1 level teaspoon salt

Main cooking utensil
saucepan

1 Put the rolled oats and water in the pan, set it aside and leave to soak overnight.
2 The following morning, add the salt and place the pan over a moderate heat.
3 With a wooden spoon, stir the porridge as it heats up so that it doesn't become lumpy.
4 When it comes to the boil, lower the heat and allow the porridge to cook very slowly for 5 minutes stirring occasionally. Turn off the heat.
5 Ladle the porridge into serving bowls and serve with brown sugar and cold milk or golden syrup.

Nutty breakfast

Muesli is a very healthful breakfast dish which you can buy in packets, but it is cheaper to make it yourself and then you can add your own favourite ingredients.

Serves 4

Ingredients
Basic mixture*
75g rolled oats
30g soft brown sugar
30g raisins or sultanas
25g flake almonds, chopped walnuts or hazelnuts
Additional ingredients
2 bananas, 2 apples or 2 fresh peaches, natural or fruit-flavoured yogurt or cold milk

1 Mix together in a bowl the rolled oats, sugar, raisins or sultanas and nuts.
2 Peel and slice the bananas; or quarter, core and chop the apples; or halve and slice the peaches.
3 Spoon 2-3 tablespoons of the basic mixture into each of four serving bowls, add the prepared fruit and pour over the yogurt or milk.

*You can make a larger amount of the basic mixture and store it in an airtight container.

Scrambled eggs on toast

Serves 4

Ingredients
6 large eggs
100ml cold milk
½ level teaspoon salt
pinch pepper
4 slices white or brown bread
butter for the toast
25g butter

Main cooking utensil
non-stick saucepan

1 Break the eggs into the basin, add the milk, salt and pepper and whisk with a fork.
2 Toast the slices of bread, spread them with butter and keep them on a plate in a warm place while you make the scrambled eggs.
3 Put the 25g of butter in a saucepan and place it over a moderate heat.
4 When the butter begins to froth, pour in the beaten egg mixture. With a wooden spoon, stir the mixture all the time so that it doesn't stick to the bottom of the pan.
5 When the mixture has just set, take the pan off the heat and spoon the scrambled egg on to the slices of toast. Remember to take the pan away from the heat as soon as the eggs have set, otherwise they will overcook and won't be as good to eat.

Poached eggs on toast

Serves 4

Ingredients
4 eggs
water
1 tablespoon vinegar
4 slices white or brown bread
butter for the toast

Main cooking utensil
frying pan

1 Pour cold water into the frying pan until it is two-thirds full and add the vinegar – this helps to hold the egg white together while the eggs are poaching.
2 Toast the slices of bread, spread each one with butter and put them on a plate in a warm place while you poach the eggs.
3 Place the pan on a moderate heat and wait for the water to come to the boil. When it boils, lower the heat. Crack each egg into a cup, and carefully drop the egg into the simmering water.
4 Leave the eggs to poach for 2-3 minutes, until they are set. Turn off the heat.
5 Take a fish slice and carefully lift each egg on to a piece of buttered toast.

Puffy bacon omelette

Serves 1

Ingredients
2 eggs
2 rashers streaky bacon
salt and pepper
2 tablespoons cold water
20g butter

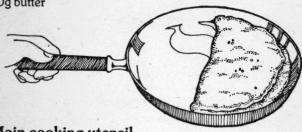

Main cooking utensil
non-stick frying pan

1 Crack the eggs and let the whites drop into one bowl and place the yolks in another.
2 With a pair of scissors cut the rinds away from the bacon, then snip the rashers into pieces and place them in a small pan.
3 Cook over a moderate heat until crisp, then remove from the heat and turn off the stove.
4 Sprinkle salt and pepper on the egg yolks, add the water and mix with a fork.
5 With an egg whisk, whisk the egg whites until they are stiff and fold them into the yoke mixture.
6 Put the butter in a non-stick frying pan and place on a moderate heat. Heat the grill.
7 When the butter begins to froth, tip in the egg mixture and spread it out with a fork to cover the bottom of the pan.
8 Cook for about 1 minute, until the mixture sets. Turn off the heat.
9 Spoon the cooked bacon over the omelette and then place it in the pan under the heated grill for about 30 seconds.
10 Fold the omelette over, then carefully lift it on to a serving plate with a fish slice.

French toast

Serves 2

Ingredients
1 egg
pinch salt
2 tablespoons cold milk
2 slices white bread
25g butter

Main cooking utensil
frying pan

1 Break the egg into shallow dish and add the salt and milk.
2 Mix the egg and milk well together with a fork.
3 Dip each slice of bread into the egg mixture so that it is coated on both sides. Place on a board.
4 Put the butter in the frying pan and place over a moderate heat.
5 When the butter melts and starts to foam add the bread slices. Cook them on one side for 1 minute, then with a fish slice turn them over to cook on the other side for 1 minute. Turn off the heat.
6 Lift the French toast on to plates and serve.

Kippers in a jug

This is a very easy way of cooking kippers. While they are in the jug you can make the toast.

Serves 2

Ingredients
2 kippers
50g butter

Main cooking utensil
earthenware jug

1 With a pair of kitchen scissors, cut the heads and tails off the kippers.
2 Place the kippers in the jug and pour in enough boiling water to cover them
3 Stand a saucer or plate on top of the jug and leave it for 10 minutes
4 Drain off the water, place each kipper on a warmed plate and top with a knob of butter

Eggs in a nest

Serves 4

Ingredients
100g butter
4 crusty rolls
4 eggs
salt and pepper

Main cooking utensil
baking tray

Before you cook.
Arrange the oven shelf on the second runner from the top and heat the oven to moderately hot (200°C, 400°F, Gas Mark 6). Lightly brush the baking tray with oil.

1 Place the butter in a small pan and put over a moderate heat until the butter has melted Turn off the heat.
2 Cut a slice from the top of each roll and using a teaspoon scoop out the middle from each one. Brush inside each scooped-out roll with the melted butter
3 Stand the rolls on the baking tray and very carefully break an egg into each one
4 Sprinkle the eggs with salt and pepper. Put them in the oven and cook for 15 minutes, until the eggs are set.
5 Put on the oven gloves, take the tray from the oven and turn the heat off
6 Serve the egg nests on a warmed plate

Bacon, eggs and fried bread

Serves 2

Ingredients
4 rashers bacon
25g lard
2 eggs
1 slice white bread

Main cooking utensil
frying pan

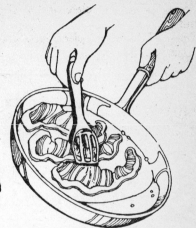

1 With a pair of kitchen scissors, cut the rinds away from the bacon.

2 Place the pan on the cooker, put in the bacon rashers and turn the heat on to moderate. Cook the rashers for 2 minutes on one side, then turn them over using a pair of tongs and cook for 2 minutes on the other side.

3 Remove the pan from the heat and place 2 rashers on each warmed serving plate. Keep them warm in a low oven or under a low grill.

4 Return the pan to the heat and add the lard. Wait until it melts then break in the eggs. When they are beginning to set, take a tablespoon and spoon the hot fat from the frying pan over the tops of the eggs to set the yolks. Remove the pan from the heat.

5 With a fish slice, place an egg on each serving plate. Keep warm.

6 Cut the slice of bread in half and place it in the pan. Return it to the heat and cook the bread for about 1 minute on each side until it is golden brown and crisp. Turn off the heat.

7 With the tongs, lift a piece of fried bread on to each serving plate. Turn off the oven or grill and serve the breakfast.

How to make tea and coffee

1 Fill the kettle with cold water and put it on to boil.

2 When the water boils, carefully pour a little into the teapot or coffee jug and leave it for a few seconds to warm the pot.

3 Tip out the water and in the teapot place 1 level teaspoon of tea per person and one for the pot; in the coffee jug put 5 level teaspoons of instant coffee powder for 600ml of water; or, if you are making ground coffee use 3 level tablespoons to 600ml of water.

4 Bring the water back to the boil and pour into the teapot or coffee jug. Put on the lid and leave for 1 minute before pouring. Don't forget to pour ground coffee and the tea through a strainer.

Breakfast tray for Mum

Mums work very hard so why not give your Mum a treat and give her breakfast in bed? You can easily do this at the weekend or when you are on holiday from school. To save time in the morning you could lay the breakfast tray the night before, but do not put out the milk or butter until the morning.

Grapefruit (see page 21)
Scrambled eggs on toast (see page 24)
Toast (see page 22)
Tea or coffee (see above)

To lay the breakfast tray
Choose a tray that is big enough to hold everything and if you like cover it with a tray cloth. On the tray place: 1 teaspoon, 1 large knife and fork, 1 small knife, 1 cup, saucer and teaspoon, sugar bowl, milk jug, side plate, toast rack, butter and marmalade in small dishes, salt and pepper and 1 napkin.

1 Prepare the grapefruit.
2 Make the toast and scrambled eggs.
3 Make the tea or coffee.

Be very careful when you are carrying the tray upstairs and hold it firmly with both hands. It is safer to make two journeys and take the tray and food up first, then come back for the tea or coffee. If the newsagent has delivered the paper and the postman has called, take the paper and letters up to Mum, too.

Main meals

Any of the recipes in this section are suitable for the main meal, which may be served in the middle of the day or in the evening. These recipes aren't difficult to make and you can serve them with a vegetable or salad depending on the time of year. At the end of each recipe in this section suggestions have been given for vegetables which could be served to make a complete meal. Instructions for preparing and cooking the vegetables will be found on pages 44 to 47.

Your main meal should always be based on protein which you need to promote growth and maintain good health. You obtain protein mostly from meat, fish, cheese, milk and eggs.

When you are planning what to cook for a main meal, remember the following points:

1 How much time you have to prepare and cook the meal.
2 The likes and dislikes of the family.
3 Choose dishes that will give a contrast in flavour, colour and texture.
4 The time of year. In the winter stews and hotpots are welcome, whereas in the summer lighter dishes are better.
5 When you have cooked the meal, serve it on warmed plates.

Tasty beef casserole

Serves 4

Ingredients
675g chuck steak
1 onion
1 carrot
2 sticks celery
226-g can tomatoes
1 beef stock cube
300ml water
2 tablespoons cooking oil
2 level tablespoons plain flour
salt and pepper

Main cooking utensil
ovenproof casserole dish

Before you cook:
Arrange the oven shelf on the centre runner and heat the oven to moderate (180°C, 350°F, Gas Mark 4).

1 First prepare the ingredients. Place the meat on a wooden board and cut it into 2·5-cm cubes, removing any fat and gristle.

Peel and slice the onion and carrot, and cut the celery sticks into 2·5-cm pieces. Open the can of tomatoes. Place the stock cube in a measuring jug and pour on 300ml boiling water.

2 Measure the oil into a frying pan and place over a moderate heat. Add the onion, carrot and celery and cook for 2 minutes. With a wooden spoon, lift the vegetables into the casserole dish.

3 Add the meat to the frying pan and fry it until it has browned on all sides. Put it in the casserole with the vegetables.

4 Remove the pan from the heat and stir in the flour, mixing it with a wooden spoon so that it blends with the fat left in the pan.

5 Return the pan to the heat and cook the flour for 1 minute, stirring. Still stirring, add the tomatoes and stock and bring the mixture to the boil. Turn off the heat.

6 Remove the pan from the heat and pour the mixture into the casserole dish. Give the ingredients a stir, add a sprinkling of salt and pepper and put the lid on the dish.

7 Put the casserole in the oven and leave it to cook for $1\frac{1}{2}$ hours.

For a complete meal serve with boiled potatoes or rice and a green vegetable (cabbage, peas or beans).

Chicken casserole

Serves 4

Ingredients
1 level tablespoon plain flour
$\frac{1}{2}$ level teaspoon salt
2 level teaspoons paprika pepper
$\frac{1}{4}$ level teaspoon cayenne pepper
4 chicken joints (defrosted if frozen ones)
425-g can tomatoes
1 onion
50g button mushrooms
50g margarine
150ml water
2 teaspoons tomato purée
1 bay leaf

Main cooking utensil
ovenproof casserole dish

Before you cook:
Arrange a shelf in the centre of the oven and heat the oven to moderate (180°C, 350°F, Gas Mark 4).

1 In a small bowl mix together the flour, salt, paprika pepper and cayenne pepper. Tip this seasoned flour into a paper bag and add one of the chicken joints. Holding the neck of the bag tightly, shake it up and down to coat the chicken joint with flour. Remove the chicken from the bag and do the same thing with the other three joints.

2 Open the can of tomatoes; peel and slice the onion and wipe the mushrooms with a piece of damp kitchen towel.
3 Put the margarine in a frying pan and place it over a moderate heat to melt. Fry the chicken joints for 3 minutes, until browned, turning them with a pair of tongs. Remove the frying pan from the heat and use the tongs to lift the chicken joints into the casserole dish.
4 Add the tomatoes, water and tomato purée to the frying pan. Return it to the heat and bring the mixture to the boil, stirring with a wooden spoon. Turn off the heat.
5 Tip the contents from the frying pan into the casserole dish and add the onion, mushrooms and bay leaf. Stir the ingredients round and cover the casserole with its lid. Place it in the oven and leave to cook for $1\frac{1}{4}$ hours.

For a complete meal serve with rice and peas.

Lamb hotpot

Serves 4

Ingredients
450g potatoes
2 onions
4 lamb chump chops or 1kg middle neck cutlets
1 level teaspoon salt
¼ level teaspoon pepper
300ml hot water
25g butter

Main cooking utensil
ovenproof casserole dish

Before you cook:
Arrange a shelf in the centre of the oven and heat the oven to moderate (180°C, 350°F, Gas Mark 4).

1 Peel and slice the potatoes and keep them in a basin covered with cold water while you prepare the other ingredients.
2 Peel and slice the onions.
3 Trim off any unwanted fat from the chops.
4 Place two of the chops, or half the number of cutlets, in the bottom of the casserole dish and sprinkle with some of the salt and pepper. On top of the chop, make a layer with half the onions, and then add a layer using half the potato slices. Sprinkle them with a little more of the salt
5 Place the other two chops, or the remaining cutlets, on top of the potatoes, add another layer of onions and finish with a top layer of potato slices. Season with the remaining salt and pepper.
6 Pour in the hot water, cover the casserole dish with its lid and cook the hotpot in the centre of the oven for 1 hour if you are using chump chops; 2-2½ hours if using middle neck cutlets.
7 Put on the oven gloves and take the casserole out of the oven. Remove the lid and dot the potatoes with the butter. Return the casserole to the oven without the lid and cook for another 15 minutes. Serve the hotpot from the casserole dish.

For a complete meal serve with carrots.

Gammon with pineapple

Serves 4

Ingredients
4 gammon rashers
227-g can pineapple rings
1 tablespoon cooking oil

Main cooking utensil
grill pan

1 With a pair of kitchen scissors, cut the rind off the gammon rashers and snip the fat at intervals to prevent the rashers from curling up during cooking. Open the can of pineapple.

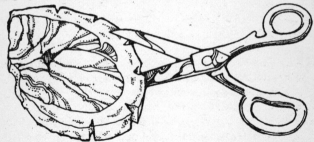

2 Brush the grill pan with oil and put the gammon in it.
3 Put the pan under the grill and turn it on to full. Cook the gammon steaks for 3 minutes, then remove the grill pan and with a pair of tongs, turn the rashers over. Replace them under the grill and cook for a further 3 minutes. (Rashers more than 5mm thick will need cooking for longer on each each side.)
4 While the gammon is cooking, place the pineapple rings and juice in a frying pan. Put over a moderate heat and cook for 2-3 minutes.
5 Arrange the gammon on a warm serving dish and with the kitchen tongs, place a ring of pineapple on each piece of gammon. Pour over the pineapple juice.

For a complete meal serve with baked tomatoes and jacket potatoes.

Pork chops with apple

Serves 4

Ingredients
4 pork loin chops
1 onion
2 tomatoes
150ml water
1 level teaspoon dried sage
salt and pepper
1 cooking apple

Main cooking utensil
ovenproof casserole dish

Before you cook:
Arrange a shelf in the centre of the oven and heat the oven to moderate (180°C, 350°F, Gas Mark 4)

1 Place the pork chops on a wooden board and with a small sharp knife trim the excess fat from the outer edge of each chop. Put the chops in the bottom of the casserole dish.
2 Peel and slice the onion. Put the tomatoes in a small basin and cover with boiling water. Leave them for 1 minute, then lift the tomatoes out with a tablespoon and peel off the skin with a small knife. Slice the tomatoes.
3 Arrange the onion and tomato slices on top of the pork chops, add the water and sprinkle the sage and seasoning over the top.
4 Cover with a lid, place in the oven and leave to cook for 1 hour.
5 While the chops are cooking, cut the apple into quarters and peel and core each quarter. Slice the quarters, place them in a bowl and cover with cold water.
6 After 1 hour, take the chops out of the oven, remove the lid from the dish and add the drained apple slices. Put the lid back on and return the dish to the oven for a further 20 minutes.
7 Serve from the casserole dish.

For a complete meal serve with baked jacket potatoes.

Sausage and onion toad-in-the-hole

Serves 6

Ingredients
1 onion
75g Cheddar cheese
2 eggs
25g lard
450g pork sausages
100g plain flour
1 level teaspoon dry mustard
½ level teaspoon salt
250ml milk

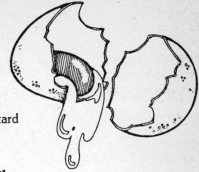

Main cooking utensil
shallow ovenproof dish

Before you cook:
Arrange the oven shelf on the second runner from the top and heat the oven to hot (220°C, 425°F, Gas Mark 7).

1 Peel and slice the onion, grate the cheese and separate the eggs into whites and yolks.
2 Put the lard, sausages and onion in the ovenproof dish and cook in the oven for 10 minutes. Pour away any excess fat.
3 Sieve the flour, mustard and salt into a mixing bowl. Make a well in the centre of the flour mixture and add the egg yolks. With a wooden spoon, gradually mix in the flour from the edges. Add the milk and continue mixing until you have made a smooth batter.
4 Place the egg whites in a bowl and whisk them until they are stiff.
5 Mix the egg whites and cheese in the batter.
6 Wearing the oven gloves, take the sausages from the oven and pour the batter over them.
7 Return the dish to the oven and cook for 30 minutes.

You don't need to serve potatoes with this dish, but baked beans would go very well.

Bacon and egg tart

Serves 6

Ingredients
Pastry
350g plain flour
$\frac{1}{4}$ level teaspoon salt
200g margarine
3 tablespoons cold water
Filling
6 rashers back bacon
4 eggs
salt and pepper
$\frac{1}{4}$ level teaspoon mixed dried herbs
2 tablespoons milk

Main cooking utensil
20-cm tart plate

Before you cook:
Arrange a shelf on the second runner in the oven and heat the oven to moderately hot (200°C, 400°F, Gas Mark 6).

1 To make the pastry, sieve the flour and salt into a mixing bowl. Cut the margarine into four pieces and add it to the sieved flour. Using your fingertips, rub the margarine into the flour until the mixture looks like breadcrumbs (see the picture on page 11). Add the water and mix it in with the blade of a knife to form a dough. Gather the dough up with your hands and place it on a floured table.
2 Divide the pastry dough in half and roll out one half with a floured rolling pin into a circle a little bit bigger than the tart plate. With the help of the rolling pin lift the circle of pastry into the tart plate and press it down with your fingertips until it lines the plate smoothly. Wash your hands and prepare the filling.
3 With a pair of kitchen scissors, cut off the bacon rinds and cut the rashers into pieces. Spread them over the pastry lining the tart plate.

4 Crack the eggs and drop the whole eggs over the bacon pieces. Sprinkle them with a little salt and pepper and the mixed dried herbs.

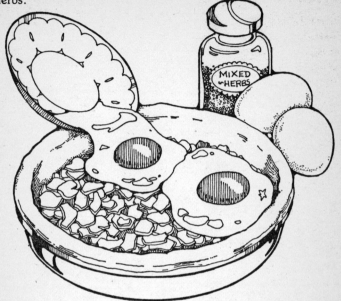

5 Now roll out the other piece of pastry dough into a circle to make a lid for the tart.

6 Brush the outer edge of the pastry lining the plate with water, and with the help of the rolling pin lift the circle of pastry over the filling.

7 Press the two pastry edges together and with a pair of scissors trim off any extra pieces of pastry. Pinch the pastry edges to make a pattern all round the edge and brush the top of the tart with milk. Make a small hole in the centre with a skewer for the steam to escape.

8 Put the tart on a baking tray, place it in the oven and cook for 40 minutes.

9 Serve hot or cold.

For a complete meal serve with runner beans.

Savoury liver and bacon bake

Serves 4

Ingredients
4 thin slices lambs' liver
1 level tablespoon plain flour
salt and pepper
1 onion
1 cooking apple
1 orange
50g butter
4 rashers back bacon

Main cooking utensil
ovenproof casserole dish

Before you cook:
Arrange a shelf in the centre of the oven and heat the oven to moderately hot (190°C, 375°F, Gas Mark 5).

1 Wash the liver slices in cold water and pat them dry with kitchen paper. Place the flour on a plate and mix in a sprinkling of salt and pepper. Coat each slice of liver on both sides with the seasoned flour.

2 Peel and slice the onion; peel, quarter, core and slice the apple and place the slices in a small basin. Cover them with cold water; cut the orange in half and squeeze out the juice.

3 Put the butter in a frying pan and place it over a moderate heat to melt. Fry the liver slices in the melted butter for 1 minute on each side, then remove the pan from the heat and with a pair of tongs, lift the liver slices into the casserole dish.

4 Add the orange juice to the pan and return it to the heat until the orange juice boils, stirring it with a wooden spoon so that all the sediment from the pan is mixed in. Turn off the heat and pour the orange juice over the liver.

5 Add the onion slices and the drained apple slices to the casserole dish.

6 Cut the rind off the bacon rashers with a pair of kitchen scissors and lay the rashers over the top of the other ingredients in the casserole.

7 Cover the dish with a lid, place it in the oven and cook for 35 minutes.
8 Serve from the casserole dish.

For a complete meal serve with rice and grilled tomatoes.

Devilled grilled fish

Serves 4

Ingredients
2 tablespoons cooking oil
4 cod steaks
100g butter
½ level teaspoon curry powder
2-3 drops Worcestershire sauce

Main cooking utensil
grill pan

Before you cook:
Heat the grill.

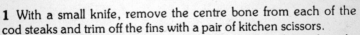

1 With a small knife, remove the centre bone from each of the cod steaks and trim off the fins with a pair of kitchen scissors.
2 Brush the grid of the grill pan with oil and place the cod steaks on it.
3 Place the butter in a small pan and put it over a moderate heat until it melts, then switch off the heat, remove the pan and stir the curry powder and Worcestershire sauce into the melted butter.
4 Brush half the melted butter mixture over the cod steaks and cook them under the grill for 3 minutes.
5 Remove the grill pan and with a fish slice turn over each steak. Brush them with the remaining butter mixture and return the pan to the grill, cooking the steaks for a further 3 minutes. Turn off the grill.
6 With the fish slice, lift the cod steaks on to a warmed serving dish.

For a complete meal serve with grilled tomatoes and potato crisps.

Vegetables

Vegetables are an important part of each meal as they supply the body with minerals, calcium and some of the essential vitamins. You should try to eat fresh vegetables at least once a day. The chart on pages 44 to 47 shows you how to prepare and cook different vegetables. When straining boiled vegetables, take care that the steam doesn't burn you. Stand the colander in the sink and holding the saucepan firmly, tip the contents through the colander. Allow the steam to disappear then tip the vegetables into a warm dish and add a knob (about 25g) of butter. If you are using frozen vegetables, read the cooking instructions on the packet. Frozen vegetables do not need to be cooked for as long as fresh vegetables as they are already partly cooked.

Vegetable	How to prepare	How to cook
Boiled potatoes	Using a potato peeler, peel away the skins and place the peeled potatoes in a bowl of cold water. If necessary, cut the potatoes into even sizes.	Half fill a pan with cold water. Add 1 teaspoon salt and the drained potatoes. Bring to the boil, cover, turn down the heat and simmer for 20-30 minutes, until soft but not mushy. Drain and serve.
Mashed potatoes	Prepare the potatoes as for boiled potatoes.	Cook the potatoes as for boiled potatoes. Drain, and return them to the pan. Add 25g butter, 2 tablespoons milk and a sprinkling of pepper. Mash with a potato masher (or a fork) until smooth. Spoon into a serving dish.

Baked jacket potatoes	Wash and scrub even-sized potatoes and prick the skin with a fork. Place on a baking tray.	Put in a moderately hot oven (200°C, 400°F, Gas Mark 6) and cook for about 1 hour, until the potatoes feel soft when squeezed. Cut a cross in the top of each potato and add a knob of butter.
Cauliflower	Break off and discard the outer leaves. Break the cauliflower into small pieces (florets) and wash in cold water. Drain.	Half fill a pan with cold water. Add 1 teaspoon of salt and bring to the boil. Add the florets, cover and cook for 15 minutes. Drain and serve.

Cabbage	With a cook's knife, cut into quarters and remove the stem. Cut each quarter into fine shreds. Wash in cold water. Drain.	Half fill a pan with cold water. Add 1 teaspoon of salt and bring to the boil. Add the cabbage, cover with a lid and cook for 10 minutes. Drain and serve.

Sprouts

With a small knife, trim away any loose leaves and cut a cross in the stem of each sprout. Leave in cold water for 10 minutes. Drain.

Half fill a pan with cold water. Add 1 teaspoon salt and bring to the boil. Add the sprouts, cover and cook for 15 minutes. Drain and serve.

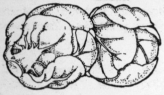

Spinach

Tear each of the leaves away from the stalks. Discard the stalks and wash the leaves very well. Drain.

Place the spinach leaves in a pan (without water), sprinkle with 1 teaspoon salt, cover with a lid and cook for 10 minutes, shaking the pan from time to time. Drain well and serve.

Leeks

With a small knife, cut a piece off the bottom and cut away the tops. Slice the leeks and wash well in cold water. Drain.

Half fill a pan with cold water. Add 1 teaspoon salt and bring to the boil. Add the leeks, cover and cook for 15 minutes. Drain and serve.

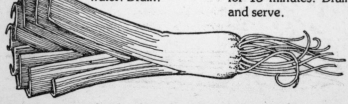

Baked tomatoes	Wipe the tomatoes, cut in half and place in an ovenproof dish. Dot each one with butter and sprinkle with salt and pepper.	Put in a moderate oven (180°C, 350°F, Gas Mark 4) and bake for 15 minutes.
Grilled tomatoes	Prepare the tomatoes as above and place them in the grill pan.	Cook under a moderate grill for about 5 minutes.
Carrots	With a small knife, cut a slice from the top and bottom of each carrot. With a potato peeler, peel away the outer skin. Cut into rounds.	Half fill a pan with cold water. Add 1 teaspoon of salt and bring to the boil. Add the carrots, cover and cook for 20 minutes. Drain and serve.
Peas	Remove the peas from their shells.	Half fill a pan with cold water. Add 1 teaspoon of salt, 1 teaspoon of sugar and a sprig of fresh mint. Bring to the boil, add the peas, cover and cook for 15 minutes. Drain and serve.

Runner beans	With a small knife, remove a piece from the top and bottom of each bean, then cut a thin strip from each side. Slice the beans diagonally into thin pieces.	Half fill a pan with cold water. Add 1 teaspoon salt and bring to the boil. Add the beans, cover and cook for 15 minutes. Drain and serve.

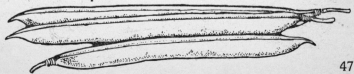

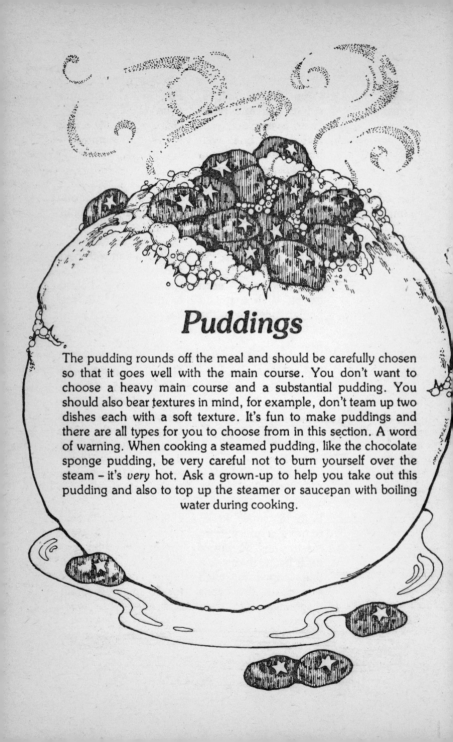

Puddings

The pudding rounds off the meal and should be carefully chosen so that it goes well with the main course. You don't want to choose a heavy main course and a substantial pudding. You should also bear textures in mind, for example, don't team up two dishes each with a soft texture. It's fun to make puddings and there are all types for you to choose from in this section. A word of warning. When cooking a steamed pudding, like the chocolate sponge pudding, be very careful not to burn yourself over the steam – it's *very* hot. Ask a grown-up to help you take out this pudding and also to top up the steamer or saucepan with boiling water during cooking.

Baked apples

Serves 4

Ingredients
4 even-sized cooking apples
50g mixed dried fruit
25g soft brown sugar
4 tablespoons golden syrup
25g butter

Main cooking utensil
shallow ovenproof dish

Before you cook:
Arrange a shelf in the centre of the oven and heat the oven to
moderately hot (200°C, 400°F, Gas Mark 6).

1 Wash the apples and remove the cores with an apple corer.
2 With a small sharp-pointed knife, slit the skins round the middle
of each apple. Stand the apples in the ovenproof dish and pour in
enough cold water to cover the bottom of the dish.

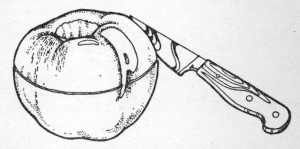

3 In a small bowl mix together the dried fruit and soft brown
sugar. Use this mixture to fill the hole in each apple – spoon it in
with a teaspoon.
4 Pour 1 tablespoon of golden syrup over each apple and put a
knob of butter on the top of each one.
5 Place in the oven and cook for 30-40 minutes until the apples
are soft. Be careful not to overcook them; if you do they will
collapse.

Chocolate fudge pudding

Serves 4

Ingredients
50g self-raising flour
25g drinking chocolate powder
75g soft margarine
75g castor sugar
1 egg
Sauce
50g soft brown sugar
15g cocoa powder
25g walnuts
2 teaspoons instant coffee powder
1 teaspoon castor sugar
300ml boiling water
Decoration
icing sugar

Main cooking utensil
pie dish

Before you cook:
Arrange a shelf in the centre of the oven and heat the oven to moderate (170°C, 325°F, Gas Mark 3). Brush all round the inside of the pie dish with a little cooking oil.

1 Sieve the flour and drinking chocolate powder into a mixing bowl. Add the soft margarine, sugar and egg.
2 With a wooden spoon, stir all the ingredients until a soft and creamy mixture is formed. Spoon this mixture into the greased pie dish.
3 In a small bowl mix together the soft brown sugar and cocoa powder. Sprinkle this over the mixture in the pie dish.
4 Put the nuts on a board, chop them with a knife, and sprinkle them over the mixture in the pie dish.
5 Spoon the instant coffee powder and castor sugar into a measuring jug. Pour on boiling water until it reaches the 300-ml mark.

6 Pour the hot black coffee over the mixture in the pie dish.

7 Place in the oven and cook for 1 hour.

8 After you have removed the pudding from the oven, sprinkle the top with icing sugar and serve hot.

N.B. This pudding is meant to be runny underneath, so don't think it isn't cooked!

Candied rice pudding

Serves 4

Ingredients
439-g can creamed rice pudding
312-g can mandarin oranges
4 level tablespoons soft brown sugar

Main cooking utensil
ovenproof dish

1 Open the cans of rice pudding and mandarin oranges and spoon the rice pudding into the ovenproof dish. Place a small sieve over a bowl and tip the mandarin oranges and juice into the sieve to drain off the juice. (You can chill the juice in the refrigerator and drink it later.)

2 Tip half the mandarin oranges into the rice pudding and with a tablespoon mix the two together. Smooth the top.

3 Sprinkle the soft brown sugar over the surface of the pudding to cover up the rice completely.

4 Turn on the grill, and when it is hot put the pudding underneath. Grill it for 2 minutes, until the sugar goes crunchy.

5 Turn off the grill, put on the oven gloves and remove the dish. Decorate the surface with the remaining mandarin orange segments.

Fruit cheesecake

Serves 8

Ingredients
225g digestive biscuits
100g margarine
Filling
2 large tubs cottage cheese
100g castor sugar
1 egg
1 lemon
Decoration
fresh raspberries, strawberries, blackberries or seedless grapes

Main cooking utensil
20-cm pie dish or fluted flan dish

Before you cook:
Arrange a shelf in the centre of the oven and heat the oven to moderately hot (190°C, 375°F, Gas Mark 5). Brush all round the inside of the baking dish with a little cooking oil.

1 Put the digestive biscuits in a polythene bag and crush them with a rolling pin until you have a bag of crumbs.

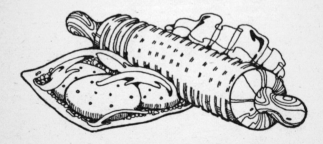

2 Put the margarine in a pan over a moderate heat until it melts, then remove the pan and turn off the heat. Tip the crumbs into the melted margarine and mix with a wooden spoon.
3 Tip the crumb mixture into the baking dish and with your fingertips press it out evenly over the base and sides of the dish.

4 Using a wooden spoon, press the cottage cheese through a sieve into a mixing bowl. Add the sugar and egg. Wash the lemon and rub it up and down the grater to grate the rind. Add the grated rind to the cottage cheese.

5 With a wooden spoon, mix all the ingredients together, then spoon the mixture into the lined baking dish. Smooth it out evenly with a small palette knife.

6 Place the cheesecake in the oven and cook for 40-45 minutes, until the filling is firm. Turn off the oven.

7 Remove the cheesecake from the oven and leave it to go cold, then decorate it with whole raspberries, strawberries or blackberries, or small bunches of seedless grapes.

Chocolate sponge pudding

Serves 4

Ingredients
100g soft margarine
100g castor sugar
2 eggs
175g self-raising flour
1½ level tablespoons cocoa powder
1 level teaspoon baking powder
4 tablespoons milk

Main cooking utensil
1·15-litre pudding basin

Before you cook:
Three-quarters fill the base of a steamer with cold water or one-third fill a large saucepan. Brush all round the inside of the pudding basin with a little cooking oil. Cut a circle of foil about 6cm larger all round than the top of the basin, and brush one side of it with oil.

1 Place the soft margarine, castor sugar and eggs in a mixing bowl. Balance a sieve over the bowl and into it put the self-raising flour, cocoa powder and baking powder. Sieve the dry ingredients into the bowl and add the milk.

2 With a wooden spoon, mix all the ingredients together until a smooth and creamy mixture is formed.

3 Spoon this mixture into the pudding basin and smooth the surface with a palette knife.

4 Cover with the foil, greased side down, and secure it under the rim of the basin.

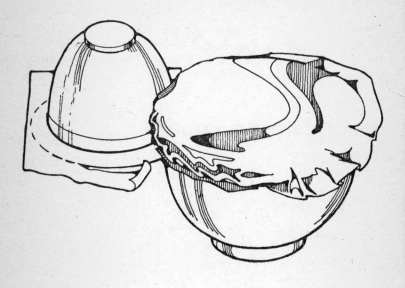

5 Allow the water to come to the boil in the steamer or saucepan. Put on the oven gloves and very carefully place the pudding basin in the steamer or pan. Cover with a lid and leave to steam for $1\frac{3}{4}$ hours, from time to time checking that there is still water in the steamer or saucepan. If not add more boiling water, wearing the oven gloves and being very careful of the hot steam.

6 After $1\frac{3}{4}$ hours turn off the heat. Put on the oven gloves and lift out the pudding basin. Take off the foil covering, and still wearing the oven gloves, turn the pudding out on to a warmed serving dish.

Bakewell tart

Serves 6

Ingredients
368-g packet frozen shortcrust pastry
3 tablespoons raspberry jam
50g margarine
50g castor sugar
2 eggs
$\frac{1}{4}$ teaspoon almond essence
50g ground almonds
Decoration
icing sugar

Main cooking utensil
20-cm pie dish or fluted flan dish

Before you cook:
Arrange a shelf in the centre of the oven and heat the oven to moderately hot (200°C, 400°F, Gas Mark 6). Allow the pastry to thaw.

1 Lightly flour the table and rolling pin and roll out the pastry to a circle a little larger than the baking dish. With the help of the rolling pin, carefully lift the pastry into the dish and press it down with your fingertips so that it lines the bottom and sides of the dish.
2 Spoon the jam on to the pastry and spread it evenly with a small palette knife.
3 Put the margarine and sugar in a mixing bowl, and mix with a wooden spoon until soft and creamy. Now add the eggs, almond essence and ground almonds and mix them in.
4 Spoon the mixture on top of the jam and spread it out evenly with the small palette knife.
5 Place in the oven and bake for 20-25 minutes until the filling has risen and is golden brown. Turn off the oven.
6 Remove from the oven, sprinkle the top with icing sugar and serve hot or cold.

Nutty fruit crumble

Serves 4

Ingredients
397-g can fruit pie filling
Crumble
175g plain flour
75g margarine
75g castor sugar
50g walnuts

Main cooking utensil
pie dish

Before you cook:
Arrange a shelf in the centre of the oven and heat the oven to moderate (180°C, 350°F, Gas Mark 4). Brush all round the inside of the pie dish with a little cooking oil.

1 Open the can of fruit pie filling and spoon the contents into the pie dish.
2 Sieve the flour into a mixing bowl. Add the margarine and with your fingertips rub it into the flour until the mixture resembles fine breadcrumbs (see page 11). With a tablespoon, stir in the sugar.
3 Put the walnuts on a board and chop them finely, then stir them into the crumble mixture.

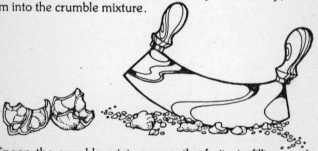

4 Spoon the crumble mixture over the fruit pie filling so that it makes an even layer.
5 Place the dish in the oven and cook for 35-40 minutes until the crumble topping is golden brown.
6 Serve hot from the pie dish.

Easy ice cream

Serves 4

Ingredients
150ml double cream
4 level tablespoons sieved icing sugar
2 egg whites

Main utensil
a shallow tray which will fit into the
freezer or freezing compartment of the
refrigerator

1 Pour the cream into a bowl and whisk until it is slightly thickened – do not over-whip or it will turn into butter.

2 Add the icing sugar and whisk it in.

3 Whisk the egg whites until stiff then fold them into the cream mixture using a metal tablespoon.

4 Pour the mixture into the shallow tray and put it in the freezer, or the freezing compartment of the refrigerator.

5 When the mixture begins to freeze around the edges take it out of the freezer, transfer it to a bowl and beat until it is smooth. Put it back into the shallow tray, return it to the freezer and freeze until firm – this usually takes about 2 hours.

6 Serve scoops of the ice cream either on its own or with your favourite canned fruit; you can also spoon some chocolate sauce (see page 58) over each serving.

Sauces to serve with puddings

With a pudding you usually serve a sweet sauce, or maybe on a special occasion, cream. The sauces described in the following pages can be served with any of the pudding recipes except candied rice pudding and cheesecake, which are served on their own. The chocolate sauce is also delicious poured over ice cream.

Custard

Serves 4

Ingredients
2 eggs
300ml cold milk
25g castor sugar

Main cooking utensil
saucepan

Before you cook:
Half fill a large pan with cold water and place on the cooker.

1 Break the eggs into a mixing bowl and with a fork, whisk them lightly. Pour in the milk and add the sugar.
2 Mix the ingredients together, then sit the mixing bowl over the saucepan.
3 Turn the heat to moderate and cook the mixture over the pan of boiling water until the custard thickens, stirring it with a wooden spoon from time to time.
4 Turn off the heat and carefully pour the custard into a warmed jug for serving.

Chocolate sauce

Serves 4

Ingredients
50g plain chocolate
4 tablespoons golden syrup
15g butter

Main cooking utensil
saucepan

Before you cook:
Half fill a saucepan with cold water and place on the cooker.

1 Break the chocolate in squares into a mixing bowl and add the golden syrup and butter.
2 Sit the mixing bowl over the saucepan. Turn on the heat and leave the ingredients to melt over the hot water, stirring from time to time.
3 Serve hot with ice cream or any chocolate pudding.

Orange or lemon sauce

Serves 4

Ingredients
1 level tablespoon cornflour
1 level tablespoon sugar
300ml milk
25g butter
2 tablespoons orange or lemon juice

Main cooking utensil
saucepan

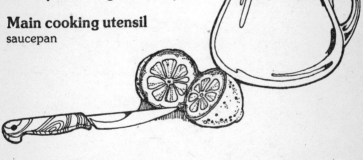

1 Put the cornflour and sugar in a small basin, add 2 tablespoons of milk and mix the ingredients to a smooth paste.
2 Pour the remaining milk into the pan, place over a moderate heat and bring to the boil.
3 Pour the heated milk over the mixture in the basin, stirring all the time.
4 Now tip the sauce back into the pan and return it to the heat. Stirring all the time, cook for 1 more minute. Turn off the heat.
5 Remove the pan from the heat and stir in the butter and orange or lemon juice.
6 Pour the sauce into a warmed jug for serving.

Baking

In this section there are recipes for biscuits, cakes, bread and teabreads – all of them easy to make. But before you start, read the following instructions which tell you about lining cake tins, how to know when cakes are cooked and how to store your cakes and biscuits – if there are any left!

Cake tins

Each recipe tells you the size of tin required and whether it should be lined with greaseproof paper. This is done to stop the cake getting overcooked on the outside before it is properly cooked in the middle. For most recipes the baking tray or cake tin should be brushed lightly with cooking oil. If you use the special non-stick utensils it isn't necessary to brush them with oil.

How to line a sandwich cake tin
1 Brush the inside of the tin with oil.
2 Cut a circle of greaseproof paper the same size as the base of the tin.
3 Place the circle in the bottom of the tin and brush the paper with cooking oil.

How to line a Swiss roll tin

1 Brush the inside of the tin with cooking oil.
2 Line the tin with a sheet of greaseproof paper that comes 1.25cm above its sides.
3 With a pair of scissors, cut into each corner of the paper, and overlap the corners to make them neat.
5 Brush the paper with oil.

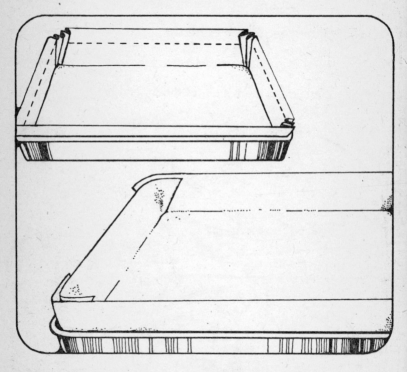

How to line a round or square deep cake tin

1 Brush all round the inside of the tin with cooking oil.
2 Cut a circle or square of greaseproof paper the same size as the bottom of the tin.
3 Cut a strip of paper 5cm deeper than the tin and big enough to go all round the inside, and fold up 5cm of the paper along one long edge.

4 With a pair of scissors, snip this fold at intervals.

5 Fit the strip into the tin with the fold at the bottom edge.

6 Put the circle in the bottom covering the snipped edges. Brush the paper with oil.

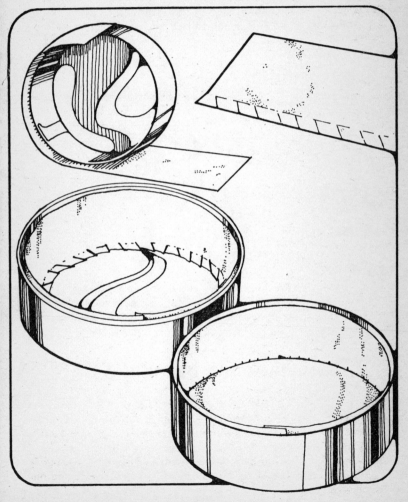

Testing a cake

The best way of testing a cake to see if it is cooked is to press it lightly with your fingertips in the centre of the top. If the surface feels firm and set the cake is cooked. (Be careful you don't burn yourself on the oven when you are doing this.) To test a big cake like the chocolate marble cake push a warmed skewer into its centre. If the skewer comes out without any cake mixture sticking to it the cake is cooked.

Cooling cakes and biscuits

When the cakes are cooked they should be turned out of the tin and left to cool on a wire tray to stop them becoming soggy. Biscuits should be lifted with a palette knife on to a wire tray for cooling.

Storing cakes and biscuits

When you have had a baking session you probably can't eat *everything* at once, but fortunately cakes and biscuits store well. Don't keep both cakes and biscuits in the same tin otherwise the cake will make the biscuits go soft. Store your cakes and biscuits in tins with tight-fitting lids, or in Tupperware containers – they are very good as they seal out all the air, which is what makes cakes and biscuits go stale.

Chocolate brownies

Makes 16 squares

One of our Test Cooks, Jason, made these in the Hamlyn Kitchen and christened them Chocolate Scouts. He thought Brownies was a soppy name.

Ingredients
50g soft margarine
75g soft brown sugar
1 egg
50g self-raising flour
2 tablespoons cocoa powder

Main cooking utensil
18-cm square shallow cake tin

Before you cook:
Brush the inside of the cake tin with a little cooking oil. Arrange a shelf on the third runner in the oven and heat the oven to moderate (180°C, 350°F, Gas Mark 4).

1 Put the margarine and sugar in a mixing bowl and beat with a wooden spoon until light and fluffy.
2 Break the egg into a cup and then add it to the mixture, beating it in well.
3 Hold a sieve over the bowl and sieve in the flour and cocoa powder. Mix it all together with the wooden spoon.
4 Spoon the mixture into the cake tin and smooth the surface with a palette knife.
5 Place the tin in the oven and cook for 25 minutes.
6 Wearing the oven gloves, take the tin out of the oven. Turn off the oven.
7 Cut the mixture into 16 small squares and let them cool in the tin for 10 minutes.
8 Take the brownies out of the tin and leave them to finish cooling on the wire tray.

Chocolate cornflake crispies

Makes 10-12 cornflake crispies

This was the favourite recipe of another of our Test Cooks, Nicola.

Ingredients
100g plain chocolate
25g margarine
25g glacé cherries
50g cornflakes
25g raisins
25g chopped nuts

Main cooking utensil
10-12 paper cases

Before you cook:
Place the paper cases on a baking tray.

1 Break up the chocolate and put it in a basin with the margarine.
2 Half fill a saucepan with cold water and place it over a moderate heat on the stove. Sit the basin on top of the saucepan until the chocolate has completely melted, stirring it from time to time with a wooden spoon. Turn off the heat.
3 With a small knife, cut each cherry in four.
4 Put the oven gloves on and lift the basin off the top of the saucepan, taking care that the hot water does not drip on you.
5 Add the cornflakes, raisins, nuts and glacé cherries to the melted chocolate and mix well with a metal tablespoon until all the cornflakes are coated with melted chocolate.
6 Put spoonfuls of the mixture in the paper cases and leave them aside to set.

Nutty chocolate cookies

Makes 10 cookies

Ingredients
25g walnuts
50g margarine
50g soft brown sugar
75g self-raising flour
1 level teaspoon cocoa powder

Main cooking utensil
2 baking trays

Before you cook:
Arrange the oven shelves on the first and second runners and heat the oven to moderately hot (190°C, 375°F, Gas Mark 5). Brush the baking trays with cooking oil.

1 Put the walnuts on a board and chop them finely.
2 Place the margarine and sugar in a mixing bowl and beat with a wooden spoon until they are very soft and well mixed.
3 Holding a sieve over the bowl, sieve in the flour and cocoa powder.
4 With a metal tablespoon mix the flour and cocoa into the margarine and sugar.
5 Finally, tip in the chopped walnuts and mix them in using the tablespoon.
6 Gather the mixture up into a ball with your hands and divide it into 10 small pieces. Form each piece into a ball.
7 Place 5 balls on each baking tray and flatten them with the prongs of a fork.
8 Put the trays in the oven and bake the cookies for 10-12 minutes.
9 Put on the oven gloves and take out the trays. Turn off the oven.
10 Allow the cookies to cool on the baking trays for 5 minutes, then lift them off with a palette knife on to a wire tray.

You could try this recipe using different kinds of nuts if you like, such as brazil nuts or almonds.

Gingerbread animals

Makes 24 gingerbread animals

Ingredients
50g soft margarine
50g castor sugar
1 tablespoon black treacle
125g self-raising flour
1 level teaspoon ground ginger
1 tablespoon milk
few currants

Main cooking utensil
2 baking trays

Before you cook:
Arrange the shelves on the second and third runners in the oven and heat it to moderate (180°C, 350°F, Gas Mark 4). Brush the baking trays with cooking oil.

1 Put the margarine and sugar in a mixing bowl and mix them together with a wooden spoon until they are light and creamy.
2 Beat in the black treacle.
3 Place a sieve over the bowl and sieve in the flour and ground ginger. Add the milk and mix all the ingredients together.
4 Sprinkle part of the table and a rolling pin with some flour. With your hands, gather the mixture into a ball and place it on the floured table. Roll it out until it is as thick as a 10p piece.
5 Cut out shapes with animal-shaped cutters and lift them on to the baking trays with a palette knife. Gather up the scraps, re-roll them and cut out more shapes. Do this until all the mixture has been used up.
6 Put a currant on each animal shape for an eye, then put the trays in the oven and bake for 15 minutes.
7 Put on the oven gloves and take out the trays. Turn off the oven. Lift the animals with a palette knife on to a wire tray to cool.

Caramel slices

Makes 18 caramel slices

Ingredients
150g self-raising flour
100g margarine
50g castor sugar
Topping
150g toffees
25g margarine
2 tablespoons milk

Main cooking utensil
15 x 22-cm shallow cake tin

Before you cook:
Arrange a shelf on the third runner of the oven and heat the oven to moderate (180°C, 350°F, Gas Mark 4). Brush the inside of the tin with cooking oil.

1 Sieve the flour into the mixing bowl. Add the margarine and with your fingertips rub it into the flour (see page 11). Then mix in the sugar.
2 Press the mixture into the cake tin and flatten it with the back of a tablespoon.
3 Put the cake in the oven and bake for 25 minutes.
4 Half fill a saucepan with water and put it over a moderate heat. Unwrap the toffees, put them in a bowl with the margarine and milk, place the bowl over the hot water and leave the toffees to melt, stirring with a wooden spoon from time to time.
5 Wearing oven gloves, take the cake tin out of the oven. Turn off the oven.
6 Remove the bowl from the pan and turn off the heat.
7 Pour the melted toffee mixture over the top of the baked mixture, smoothing the surface with a palette knife.
8 Leave in the refrigerator for 30 minutes for the topping to set, then cut into 18 slices and remove from the tin.

Orange shortbread round

Ingredients
1 orange
75g soft butter
4 level tablespoons icing sugar
125g plain flour
2 teaspoons castor sugar

Main cooking utensil
18-cm sandwich cake tin

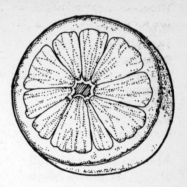

Before you cook:
Arrange a shelf on the bottom runner of the oven and heat the
oven to moderate (180°C, 350°F, Gas Mark 4). Brush the inside
of the sandwich tin with cooking oil.

1 Wash the orange and grate the rind on to a piece of kitchen
paper.
2 Put the butter in the mixing bowl, then sieve in the icing sugar.
3 Add the orange rind and mix the ingredients together with a
wooden spoon until they are light and fluffy.
4 Hold the sieve over the bowl again and sieve the flour into the
mixture. Mix together all the ingredients and with your hands
form them into a dough.
5 Press the dough into the oiled tin so that it covers the bottom
evenly, and prick it all over with the fork. Mark the edges lightly
with the prongs of the fork.
6 Mark the shortbread round into eight triangles and place in the
oven. Bake for 35 minutes, until the shortbread is a pale golden
colour.
7 Put on the oven gloves and take the shortbread out. Turn off
the oven.
8 Leave the shortbread to cool for 10 minutes in the tin then turn
the tin upside down over the wire tray and let the cake fall out.
With a palette knife, turn the shortbread the right way up and
sprinkle the surface with castor sugar. When cool, cut into the
eight pieces.

Chocolate marble cake

Chocolate marble cake looks very pretty when you cut it as you see some plain and some chocolate cake in each piece.

Ingredients
100g self-raising flour
1 level teaspoon baking powder
100g castor sugar
100g soft margarine
2 eggs
3 level tablespoons cocoa powder

Main cooking utensil
18-cm deep round cake tin

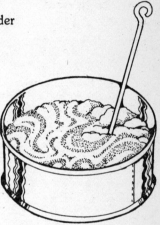

Before you cook:
Arrange a shelf in the centre of the oven and heat the oven to moderately hot (190°C, 375°F, Gas Mark 5). Brush the inside of the tin with cooking oil.

1 Sieve the flour and baking powder into the mixing bowl. Add the sugar, margarine and eggs, and with a wooden spoon mix all the ingredients together until they are soft and creamy.
2 Drop spoonfuls of half the mixture into the tin.
3 Sieve the cocoa powder into the rest and stir it in to make a chocolate mixture.
4 Now drop spoonfuls of the chocolate mixture into the cake, between the blobs of plain mixture. Run a skewer through the mixture to blend, but not mix, the colours.

5 Smooth the surface and put the cake in the oven. Bake for 45 minutes.
6 Put on the oven gloves and take the cake out of the oven. Turn off the oven.
7 Leave the cake in the tin for 5 minutes, then turn it on to a wire tray to finish cooling.

Butterfly buns

Makes 18 butterfly buns

Ingredients
100g self-raising flour
1 level teaspoon baking powder
100g soft margarine
100g castor sugar
2 eggs
Icing
100g icing sugar
1 tablespoon milk
50g soft margarine
few jelly sweets

Main cooking utensil
18 paper cases

Before you cook:
Arrange the oven shelves on the second and third runners and heat the oven to moderately hot (190°C, 375°F, Gas Mark 5). Separate the paper cases and arrange them on 2 baking trays.

1 Sieve the flour and baking powder into a mixing bowl, then add the margarine, sugar and eggs. With a wooden spoon mix all the ingredients together until they are light and creamy.
2 Put a teaspoonful of the mixture in each paper case.
3 Place the trays in the oven and bake for 15 minutes.
4 Wearing the oven gloves, remove the trays from the oven and leave the buns to cool in their cases. Turn off the oven.

5 Sieve the icing sugar into a clean bowl. Add the milk and margarine and mix together with a wooden spoon to make the icing.

6 When the buns are cold, carefully cut a circle out of the top of each one and set it aside.

7 Fill the hole in each bun with a teaspoonful of icing.

8 Cut each of the circles that you removed in half and put the two halves back on each bun, with the tops slanted slightly to look like wings.

9 Put a jelly sweet in the centre of each bun, between the wings.

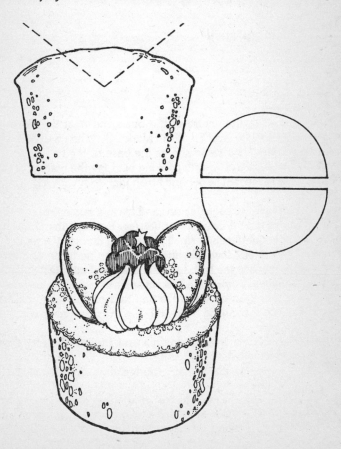

Apple and raisin teabread

Ingredients
100g margarine
100g castor sugar
50g raisins
300ml cold tea without milk
1 apple
225g self-raising flour
1 level teaspoon bicarbonate of soda
½ level teaspoon salt

Main cooking utensil
900-g loaf tin

Before you cook:
Arrange a shelf in the centre of the oven and heat the oven to moderate (180°C, 350°F, Gas Mark 4). Cut a piece of greaseproof paper the same size as the base of the tin. Brush all round the inside of the tin with cooking oil. Line the bottom of the tin with the greaseproof paper and brush that, too, with oil.

1 Put the margarine, sugar, raisins and tea in a saucepan.
2 Peel the apple and cut it into quarters. Remove the core and chop the apple quarters into small pieces. Put them in the pan.
3 Put the pan over a low heat and stir with a wooden spoon until the mixture comes to the boil. Let it simmer for 4 minutes.
4 Sieve the flour, bicarbonate of soda and salt into a mixing bowl.
5 Take the saucepan off the stove and turn off the heat. Tip the hot mixture into the mixing bowl and with the wooden spoon mix all the ingredients together.
6 Spoon the mixture into the loaf tin and smooth the top, then put it in the oven to bake for 1¼ hours.
7 Wearing the oven gloves, take the teabread out of the oven. Turn off the oven.
8 Leave the teabread in the tin for 10 minutes, then turn out on to a wire tray. Peel off the paper and finish cooling.
9 Serve sliced and spread with butter.

Lemon loaf

Ingredients
200g self-raising flour
1 level teaspoon baking powder
1 level teaspoon salt
75g margarine
3 lemons
50g castor sugar
milk
2 eggs

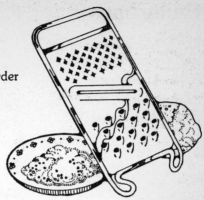

Main cooking utensil
450-g loaf tin

Before you cook:
Arrange a shelf in the centre of the oven and heat the oven to moderate (180°C, 350°F, Gas Mark 4). Cut a piece of greaseproof paper the same size as the base of the loaf tin. Brush all round the inside of the tin with cooking oil, place the greaseproof paper in the bottom and brush that, too, with oil.

1 Sieve the flour, baking powder and salt into a mixing bowl.
2 Add the margarine, and with your fingertips rub it in until the mixture looks like breadcrumbs.
3 Wash the lemons and grate the rind into the mixing bowl. Add the sugar. Squeeze the juice from the lemons and put it into a measuring jug. Pour in enough milk to come up to the 125-ml mark.
4 Add the eggs to the liquid and mix them in with a fork.
5 Tip the liquid into the mixing bowl and with a tablespoon mix all the ingredients together to form a dough.
6 Spoon the dough into the loaf tin and smooth the top.
7 Place in the oven and bake for 45-50 minutes.
8 Put on the oven gloves and take the loaf out of the oven. Turn off the oven.
9 Leave the loaf in the tin for 10 minutes, then turn it on to a wire tray. Peel off the paper and finish cooling.
10 Serve sliced and spread with butter.

Fruity baps

Bread making is very easy if you use a bread mix, which you can buy from most supermarkets.

Makes 8 fruity baps

Ingredients
275g white bread mix
100g sultanas
200ml hot water

Main cooking utensil
baking tray

Before you cook:
Arrange a shelf in the centre of the oven and heat the oven to very hot (230°C, 450°F, Gas Mark 8). Brush the baking tray with cooking oil.

1 Tip the bread mix and sultanas into a mixing bowl, add the hot water and mix with a wooden spoon to form a dough.
2 Sprinkle the table top with flour. Take the dough out of the bowl and knead it with your hands for 5 minutes.
3 Divide the dough into 8 equal-sized pieces and with your hands shape each piece into a nice, neat round. Put the rounds on the baking tray. Cover with a damp, clean tea towel and leave in a warm place for 35 minutes to rise.
4 Remove the tea towel and place the baps in the oven; cook for 15 minutes.
5 Wearing the oven gloves, take the baps out of the oven. Turn off the oven, and with a palette knife lift the baps on to a wire tray to cool.
6 Serve the baps split in half and spread with butter.

Bread mice

Makes 8 bread mice

Ingredients
275g white bread mix
200ml hot water

Main cooking utensil
baking tray

Before you cook:
Arrange a shelf in the centre of the oven and heat the oven to very hot (230°C, 450°F, Gas Mark 8). Brush the baking tray with cooking oil.

1 Put the bread mix in a mixing bowl and add the hot water. Mix with a wooden spoon to form a dough.
2 Sprinkle the table top with flour. Take the dough out of the bowl and knead it with your hands for 5 minutes.
3 Cut the dough in half and divide one half into 8 equal-sized pieces. Shape these 8 pieces into round mouse-bodies and put them on the baking tray.
4 Divide the rest of the dough in half and from one half shape 8 heads. Press these on to the bodies.
5 From the remainder of the dough make 8 long thin tails and 16 small round ears. Press a tail and two ears into each mouse.

6 Cover the baking tray with a clean, damp tea towel and leave in a warm place for 35 minutes.
7 Remove the cloth and put the tray in the oven to bake for 15 minutes.
8 Put on the oven gloves and take the tray out of the oven. Turn off the oven.
9 With a palette knife lift the bread mice on to a wire tray to cool.
10 Serve the mice with butter.

Presents to make

This section gives you ideas for little gifts you can make at home, for Christmas or birthday presents, and there is even a special Mothers' Day cake so you can give your Mum a delicious surprise on Mothers' Day.

To make your home-made sweets into an attractive present, wrap them individually in pieces of cling film and then pack a selection in a pottery mug with a piece of ribbon tied on the handle. Another way is to put the sweets in individual sweet paper cases (which you can buy from a stationer's) and pack them in a small box. Cover the box with coloured cellophane paper and secure it with ribbon.

Fruit fudge

Makes 49 pieces of fudge

Ingredients
100g margarine
150ml evaporated milk
450g granulated sugar
$\frac{1}{2}$ teaspoon vanilla essence
pinch cream of tartar
25g sultanas

Main cooking utensil
thick-bottomed saucepan

Before you cook:
Brush all round the inside of an 18-cm square tin with cooking oil.

When you are making this fruit fudge you must ask a grown-up to be in the kitchen because the sugar mixture gets very hot and you must be very careful indeed not to splash any on you.

1 Place the margarine, evaporated milk, sugar, vanilla essence and cream of tartar in the pan.
2 Put over a moderate heat and stir with a wooden spoon until the sugar has dissolved.
3 Let the mixture come to the boil and allow it to boil for 10 minutes. **The mixture is now very hot, so take great care!**
4 Ask the grown-up to drop a little of the mixture into a cup of cold water to test if it is ready. If so, it will form a soft ball.
5 Turn off the heat and carefully lift the pan on to a wooden board.
6 Beat the mixture with a wooden spoon for 2-3 minutes, again being careful not to splash, then stir in the sultanas.
7 Pour the fudge into the tin. When it is almost set cut it into 49 squares and leave to set completely.

Peppermint creams

Makes about 50 peppermint creams

Ingredients
25g margarine
1 tablespoon milk
225g icing sugar
few drops peppermint essence
few drops green food colouring

Main cooking utensil
small saucepan

1 Place the margarine and milk in the pan and put over a moderate heat until the margarine melts, then turn off the heat and remove the pan.
2 Sieve the icing sugar into a mixing bowl and pour on the melted ingredients. Add the peppermint essence and green food colouring and mix everything together with a spoon, then gather the mixture up with your hands.
3 Sprinkle part of the table top with a little icing sugar and knead the mixture – it should feel soft and silky.
4 With a rolling pin roll out the mixture to a 5mm thickness and cut it into rounds with a 2·5-cm plain cutter. As you cut out the rounds lay them flat on a sheet of greaseproof paper to harden. Gather up the scraps, knead them together and roll out the mixture again. Do this until it is all used up.

Coconut ice

Makes about 675g coconut ice

Ingredients
1 small can condensed milk
250g icing sugar
175g desiccated coconut
few drops red food colouring

1 Open the can of condensed milk and pour it into a mixing bowl. Place a sieve over the bowl and sieve in the icing sugar, then mix the two together with a wooden spoon.

2 Add the coconut and stir it in. The mixture should be very stiff.

3 Divide the mixture in half. To one half add a few drops of red food colouring and with your hands knead the mixture until it is an even colour.

4 Shape the pink and white mixtures into two bars, press them together and leave until firm.

5 When set, cut the bars into squares.

Easy chocolate fudge

Makes about 50 squares of fudge

Ingredients

100g plain chocolate
50g margarine
450g icing sugar
1 teaspoon vanilla essence
3 tablespoons single cream

Main cooking utensil

saucepan

Before you cook:
Brush all round the inside of a 20-cm square cake tin with oil.

1 Break the chocolate into squares into the pan and add the margarine. Place the pan over a moderate heat and stir the ingredients together with a wooden spoon until they have melted. Turn off the heat and remove the pan.

2 Sieve the icing sugar into a mixing bowl and pour in the melted ingredients. Add the vanilla essence and cream and with the wooden spoon mix everything well together.

3 Spoon the mixture into the tin, smooth the surface and leave it to set in a cool place.

4 When completely set, cut into small squares.

Mothers' Day cake

Ingredients
25g angelica
100g glacé cherries
25g crystallised ginger
1 orange
100g blanched almonds
175g margarine
175g castor sugar
3 eggs
225g plain flour
1 level teaspoon mixed spice
225g raisins
2 tablespoons milk

Topping
6 walnut halves
halved glacé cherries
5 brazil nuts
1 tablespoon apricot jam

Main cooking utensil
18-cm round cake tin

Before you cook:
Arrange a shelf in the centre of the oven and heat to very cool (140°C, 275°F, Gas Mark 1). Brush all round the inside of the tin with a little cooking oil. Line the bottom and sides of the tin with greaseproof paper and brush the paper with oil.

1 Cut the angelica, glacé cherries and crystallised ginger into small pieces. Wash the orange and grate the rind on to a piece of kitchen paper. Chop the almonds.
2 Place the margarine and castor sugar in a mixing bowl and with a wooden spoon beat together until the mixture is light and creamy.
3 Break one egg into the creamed mixture and beat it in. Then beat the second one in. Add 1 tablespoon of the flour, then break the third egg in. Beat it in well.
4 Sieve the remaining flour and the mixed spice into the mixing

bowl. Add the raisins, orange rind, angelica, glacé cherries, almonds, ginger and milk.

5 Using a metal tablespoon, carefully mix all the ingredients together.

6 Spoon the mixture into the cake tin, smoothing the surface with the back of the tablespoon.

7 Place the walnut halves around the cake edge, then make a circle of halved glacé cherries. In the centre arrange the brazil nuts in a flower pattern.

8 Place the cake in the oven and bake for $3-3\frac{1}{4}$ hours. Turn off the oven.

9 Put on the oven gloves and remove the cake from the oven. Leave it in the tin for 5 minutes, then turn it out on to a wire tray and peel off the paper.

10 Brush the surface of the warm cake with apricot jam to make it shiny, then leave it to cool.

Eggs for Easter

These are fun to do and really brighten up breakfast if placed in a pretty basket and put in the centre of the table on Easter Sunday morning. You can do an egg for each member of the family with his or her name on it.

Put the eggs in a pan and cover with cold water. Place on a moderate heat, bring to the boil and boil for 10 minutes. Turn off the heat and lift out the eggs with a tablespoon. Allow them to cool slightly then brush each one all over with a coating of lightly-beaten egg white. When the coating has dried you can write a name or draw a pattern or a funny face on each egg with coloured felt-tipped pens.

Feeding your friends

During the holidays, or when you come home from school with some of your friends and it is too wet to go outside, why don't you have a cooking session in the kitchen? Some of the recipes in this section are savoury, others are sweet, but they are all fun to make – and delicious to eat!

Sandwich boats

Makes 6 boats

Ingredients
6 frankfurters
6 long rolls
butter
3 slices processed cheese
3 tomatoes
6 cocktail sticks

Main cooking utensil
saucepan

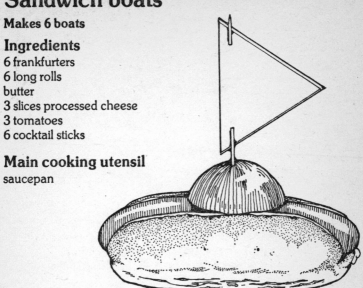

1 Put the frankfurters in the pan and cover with cold water. Place over a moderate heat and when the water boils, lower the heat and leave the frankfurters to cook for 10 minutes. Then turn off the heat, and with a pair of kitchen tongs lift the frankfurters on to a plate to cool.

2 Cut each roll along the top, but do not cut it right through. Spread the insides with butter and place a frankfurter in each one.

3 Cut each slice of cheese in half from corner to corner to make two triangles.

4 Push a cocktail stick into one corner of each triangle of cheese and bring it out again at one of the other corners so that the cheese is fastened on to the stick.

5 Cut the tomatoes in halves and push one half on to each cocktail stick next to the cheese.

6 Push a cocktail stick into each frankfurter so that the tomato is next to the frankfurter. You have now got sandwich boats which you can eat!

Home-made hamburgers

Serves 4

Ingredients
1 small onion
450g lean minced beef
½ level teaspoon salt
¼ level teaspoon pepper
pinch dried mixed herbs
2 tablespoons cooking oil
4 baps

Main cooking utensil
frying pan

1 Peel and chop the onion finely.
2 In a basin place the onion, minced beef, salt, pepper and mixed herbs and with a spoon mix all the ingredients together.
3 With your hands divide the mixture into four portions and shape each portion into a round, flat cake.
4 Pour the oil into the frying pan and heat on the top of the cooker. Fry the burgers for 5 minutes on each side, turning them with a fish slice. Turn off the heat.
5 Cut the baps almost in half and place a burger in each one. Serve with tomato ketchup.

Beany nests

Makes 2 nests

Ingredients
250ml boiling water
220-g can baked beans
50g Cheddar cheese
64-g packet instant potato

Main cooking utensil
baking tray

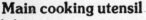

Before you cook:
Arrange a shelf in the centre of the oven and heat the oven to moderately hot (200°C, 400°F, Gas Mark 6). Lightly brush the baking tray with cooking oil.

1 Put the kettle of water on to boil. When it boils, pour 250ml of boiling water into a measuring jug. Open the can of beans. Grate the cheese on to a piece of kitchen paper.
2 Tip the instant potato into a small basin and pour on the boiling water. Mix with a fork to make mashed potato.
3 Divide the potato into two piles on the baking tray. With the back of a tablespoon make a well in the centre of each pile, and fill it with baked beans.
4 Sprinkle the grated cheese over each nest.
5 Place in the oven and bake for 25 minutes.
6 Put on the oven gloves and remove the tray from the oven. Turn off the oven.
7 With a palette knife lift the beany nests on to a plate and eat them hot.

Crispy corned beef savoury

Serves 4

Ingredients
250ml boiling water
198-g can corned beef
64-g packet instant potato
1 small packet cheese and onion crisps

Main cooking utensil
ovenproof dish

Before you cook:
Arrange a shelf in the centre of the oven and heat the oven to moderately hot (200°C, 400°F, Gas Mark 6). Lightly brush the inside of the ovenproof dish with cooking oil.

1 Put a kettle of water on to boil. When it boils pour 250ml into a measuring jug. Open the can of corned beef.
2 Tip the instant potato into a basin and pour on the boiling water. Mix with a fork to make mashed potato.
3 Turn the corned beef out on to a board and cut it into small pieces. Put it in the bowl with the mashed potato and mix the two together.
4 Spoon the mixture into the ovenproof dish and press it well down. Before you open the bag of crisps press it between your hands to crush them, then open the bag and sprinkle the crisps over the top of the corned beef mixture.
5 Put the corned beef savoury in the oven and cook for 20 minutes. Turn off the oven.
6 Put on the oven gloves and take the dish out of the oven. Serve from the dish on to plates.

Biscuit layer trifle

Serves 4

Ingredients
8 digestive biscuits
50g butter or margarine
25g castor sugar
397-g can fruit pie filling – your favourite variety
1 small can evaporated milk

Main cooking utensil
saucepan

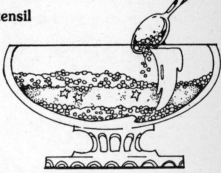

1 Put the digestive biscuits in a clean polythene bag and crush them with a rolling pin.
2 Put the butter in the saucepan and place over a moderate heat to melt. When melted, turn off the heat and remove the pan.
3 Tip the biscuit crumbs into the melted butter and add the sugar. Mix the ingredients together with a wooden spoon. Now open the cans of pie filling and evaporated milk.
4 Spread half the biscuit mixture in the bottom of a glass bowl, then spread over half the pie filling. Add the rest of the biscuit mixture.
5 Put the other half of the pie filling in a basin, add the evaporated milk and mix them well together.
6 Spoon this mixture into the glass bowl, making a smooth layer.
7 Place in the refrigerator for 15 minutes to chill. While the trifle is chilling you can quickly do the washing up so there will be nothing to mar your enjoyment when you and your friends eat the trifle later!

Marshmallow dip

Ingredients
150g pink and white marshmallows
2 tablespoons milk

Main cooking utensil
saucepan

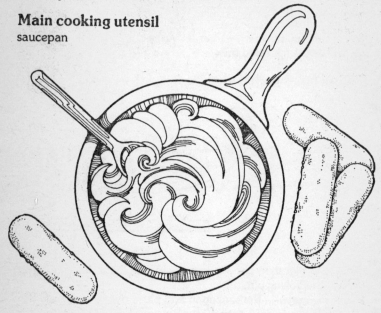

1 Half fill the saucepan with cold water and place it over a moderate heat.

2 Put the marshmallows in a bowl which will fit over the saucepan. Add the milk, and place the bowl on the saucepan.

3 Leave the marshmallows to melt, stirring the mixture from time to time with a wooden spoon.

4 When melted, remove the basin from the heat, taking care not to scald yourself with the steam from the pan, and turn off the cooking ring. Beat the mixture with the wooden spoon for 1 minute.

5 Put sponge finger biscuits, pieces of broken biscuit or small crackers out for you and your friends to dip into the marshmallow mixture while it is still warm.

Toffee crisps

Makes 12 toffee crisps

Ingredients
50g caramel toffees
25g rice krispies
50g plain chocolate
1 orange

Main cooking utensil
saucepan

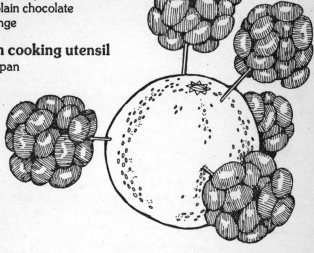

1 Half fill the· saucepan with cold water and place over a moderate heat. Unwrap the toffees, put them in a bowl which will fit over the saucepan, and leave the bowl over the pan until the toffees have melted. Turn off the heat and remove the bowl from the pan, again being careful of the steam.
2 Add the rice krispies to the melted toffees and stir with a wooden spoon until the krispies are coated with toffee.
3 With your hands, make the mixture into 12 balls and push a cocktail stick into each one.
4 Break the chocolate into a clean bowl, sit the bowl over the pan and turn on the heat until the chocolate melts. When melted, turn off the heat and carefully remove the bowl.
5 Holding each crisp by the cocktail stick, dip it into the melted chocolate, then stick it in the orange and leave until the chocolate has set. Be careful not to let the crisps touch one another once they have been dipped in the chocolate.

Here are some ideas for snacks which are very quick to make – ideal for times when you are in a hurry to go out again.

Teatime toasts

Toast, served hot and spread with lots of butter, makes a delicious teatime treat. But why not add a topping as well? Here are some suggestions for extra-special toast.

Cinnamon toast
In a small basin mix together 1 tablespoon ground cinnamon and 3 tablespoons castor sugar. Make the toast and spread with butter, then sprinkle with the cinnamon mixture. Cut into fingers and serve.

Sardines
Open a can of sardines – you may have to ask a grown-up to help as these cans are often tricky – tip the sardines and oil into a basin and add a shake of black pepper. Mash the sardines with a fork, then spread over slices of hot buttered toast. Cut into fingers and serve.

Marmite and cheese
Grate some Cheddar cheese on to a piece of kitchen paper. Make the toast and spread with butter. Now spread with a *thin* layer of Marmite, then cover with the grated cheese. Put the toast back under the grill to melt the cheese, then remove, cut into fingers and serve.

Open sandwiches

These sandwiches originated in Scandinavia. Unlike our traditional sandwiches they do not have two layers of bread with a filling in-between. Instead, there is a base which can be crisp-bread, toast or ordinary bread (usually brown), spread with butter, to which various toppings are added, and the sandwiches are made colourful with a variety of garnishes. Here are some suggested toppings, but you can invent your own, depending on what foods are available, and what you like best. Open sandwiches are usually eaten with a knife and fork as they are a bit difficult to manage otherwise.

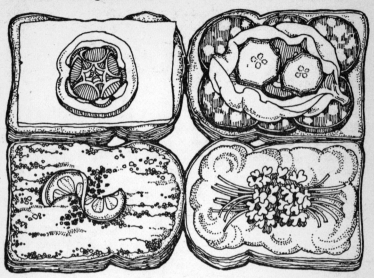

Open sandwich toppings

1 Place thin slices of cheese on the base and garnish with tomato rings, halved grapes or slices of radish.

2 Spread the base with cream cheese, sprinkle with chopped walnuts and garnish with a slice of orange.

3 Spread the base with chopped hard-boiled egg mixed with salad cream and chopped parsley; garnish with cress.

4 Place thin slices of cooked cold meat (ham, beef, pork or salami) on the base and garnish with a lettuce leaf and tomato and cucumber slices.

5 Spread the base with mashed sardines and garnish with a slice of lemon and a sprig of parsley.

6 Spread pâté on the base and garnish with onion and tomato rings and parsley.

7 Spread the base with cooked chopped chicken mixed with salad cream or mayonnaise and garnish with watercress.

Ginger beer

This fizzy drink can be made very easily at home providing you are patient, as you have to feed the mixture once a day for 6 days before you can bottle it, and then you have to leave it for another 7 days before you can drink it. Do make sure that you use strong bottles with screw tops.

Ingredients

The starter
15g dried yeast
450ml warm water
2 level teaspoons ground ginger
2 level teaspoons castor sugar
To feed the mixture
6 level teaspoons ground ginger
6 level teaspoons castor sugar
To flavour
675g castor sugar
1·15 litres water
juice of 2 lemons
To dilute
3 litres water

1 Place the ingredients for the starter in a mixing bowl and mix with a wooden spoon. Cover with a clean tea towel and leave in a warm place for 24 hours.
2 Stir 1 level teaspoon of ground ginger and 1 level teaspoon of castor sugar into the mixture each day.
3 After 7 days, strain the mixture through a sieve lined with muslin into a large clean bowl.

4 Now place the sugar and water in a saucepan over a moderate heat until the sugar dissolves.

5 Pour the sugar solution into the strained mixture. Add the lemon juice and dilute the mixture with 3 litres of cold water.

6 Leave the ginger beer to cool, then pour it into clean, strong bottles. Secure the screw tops, then store the bottles in a cool place for 7 days. It's a good idea to label the bottles with the date the beer is ready for drinking.

Banana milk shake

Serves 4

Ingredients
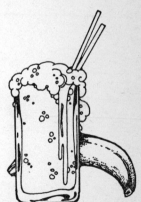
1 banana
2 teaspoons honey
4 tablespoons vanilla ice cream
1 small carton fruit yogurt
600ml milk

1 Peel the banana and place it in a mixing bowl. Mash with a fork and mix in the honey.

2 Add the ice cream and mix it in until softened.

3 Whisk in the yogurt and milk, and serve at once in tumblers.

Cooking for special occasions

All through the year there are days when we eat special dishes – for example at Easter and Christmas – but there are also times like birthdays and other celebrations with our family or friends when it's fun to make an unusual cake or other dish. Although the recipes in this section are designed for these occasions, they are no more difficult to make than the others in this book.

Easter biscuits

Makes approximately 36 biscuits

Ingredients
100g margarine
100g castor sugar
200g plain flour
½ level teaspoon mixed spice
100g currants
1 egg

Main cooking utensil
2 baking trays

Before you cook:
Arrange the oven shelves on the first and second runners and heat the oven to moderate (180°C, 350°F, Gas Mark 4). Brush the baking trays with cooking oil.

1 Put the margarine and sugar in a mixing bowl and with a wooden spoon, beat the mixture until it is light and creamy in appearance.
2 Sieve in the flour and mixed spice and work them into the creamed mixture with the wooden spoon.
3 Now add the currants and egg and mix with the wooden spoon to form a dough.
4 Turn the dough on to a floured table and knead it with your hands. Flour the rolling pin and roll out the dough to the thickness of a 10p piece.
5 With a 6-cm fluted cutter cut out circles from the dough and place on the baking trays. Gather up the scraps of dough, knead them and roll them out again and cut out more biscuits. Do this until all the dough is used up.
6 Put the baking trays in the oven and cook the biscuits for 10 minutes. Change the trays around and cook for a further 5 minutes until all the biscuits are lightly golden in colour. Turn off the oven.
7 Put on the oven gloves, take out the trays and with a palette knife, lift the bicuits on to a wire tray to cool.

Hot cross buns

Traditionally, these buns are eaten for breakfast on Good Friday.

Makes 8 hot cross buns

Ingredients
125ml milk
1 level teaspoon castor sugar
1½ level teaspoons dried yeast
250g strong plain flour*
½ level teaspoon salt
1 level teaspoon mixed spice
25g margarine
50g castor sugar
25g dried fruit
1 egg
Glaze
1 level tablespoon castor sugar
1 tablespoon water

Main cooking utensil
baking tray

Before you cook:
Arrange the oven shelf on the second runner from the top and heat the oven to hot (220°C, 425°F, Gas Mark 7). Lightly brush the baking tray with a little cooking oil.

1 Pour the milk into a pan and place it over a moderate heat until warm – but do not let it get too hot. Turn off the heat and remove the pan.

2 In a small bowl place the warm milk, 1 teaspoon castor sugar and the dried yeast. Leave for 10-15 minutes, until the mixture looks frothy.

3 Sieve the flour, salt and mixed spice into a mixing bowl. Add the margarine and rub it in with your fingertips until the mixture looks like breadcrumbs.

*This is a special kind of plain flour used in yeast recipes such as bread and buns. If you haven't got any, you can use ordinary plain flour.

4 Now stir in the sugar and dried fruit.

5 Make a hole in the centre of the mixture and break in the egg. Pour in the frothy yeast mixture, and with a wooden spoon, work all the ingredients together to form a dough. Beat the dough well for 2 minutes.

6 Cover the mixing bowl with a clean tea towel and leave it in a warm place for about 1 hour to rise.

7 When the dough has risen, turn it out on to a floured table and knead it with your hands – it should feel soft and elastic. Divide the dough into eight equal-sized pieces. Lightly flour your hands and shape each piece of dough into a round. Place the rounds on the baking tray and flatten each one slightly with the palm of your hand. With a sharp knife, mark a cross on each bun.

8 Put the tea towel over the tray of buns and leave them in a warm place until they have become twice their original size – this takes 15-20 minutes.

9 Put the tray of buns in the oven and bake them for 15-20 minutes, until golden brown.

10 Meanwhile, make the glaze. Measure the castor sugar and water into a small pan and place over a moderate heat until the sugar has dissolved. Turn off the heat.

11 Put on the oven gloves and take the buns out of the oven. Turn off the oven.

12 Brush the hot buns with the glaze to make them shiny. Serve warm.

Iced birthday cake

Ingredients
3 eggs
75g castor sugar
75g plain flour
½ level teaspoon baking powder
Filling
2 level tablespoons strawberry jam
Icing
100g icing sugar
2 tablespoons hot water

Main cooking utensil
20-cm sandwich cake tin

Before you cook:
Arrange the oven shelf on the middle runner and heat the oven to moderate (180°C, 350°F, Gas Mark 4). Brush all round the inside of the tin with a little cooking oil. Cut a circle of greaseproof paper the same size as the base of the tin and fit it into the tin. Brush the paper with oil. Sprinkle a little flour inside the tin, shake it to distribute the flour evenly and tip out any surplus. Place a saucepan half filled with cold water on the cooker.

1 Break the eggs into a mixing bowl and add the sugar.
2 Place the bowl over the pan of water and turn the heat on to moderate. With a rotary whisk, whisk the eggs and sugar over the hot water until the mixture becomes thick and lighter in colour – this will take 10-15 minutes. From time to time, take a spatula and scrape the mixture down from the sides of the bowl so that it becomes evenly mixed. If you find that the bowl on top of the saucepan is too high for you to whisk the mixture comfortably, stand on a stool, but be very careful and make sure the stool is steady.
3 Turn off the heat and lift the mixing bowl on to the table, placing it on a damp dish-cloth to stop it from slipping. Whisk the mixture for another 5 minutes. This is hard work, but unless you whisk it properly your cake will be heavy.
4 Sieve the flour and baking powder into the mixture, then take a

metal tablespoon and *very gently* fold in the flour until it is all mixed in.

5 Spoon the mixture into the prepared cake tin and smooth the surface.

6 Put the tin in the oven and cook for 30-35 minutes, until the cake is risen, lightly browned and firm to the touch in the centre. Turn off the oven.

7 Put on the oven gloves, take the cake out and turn it out on to a wire tray to cool. Peel off the paper.

8 When the cake is cool cut it in half horizontally and spread one half with the strawberry jam. Put the two halves back together and place the cake on a plate lined with a pretty doily.

9 Sieve the icing sugar into a small basin and add the hot water. Mix it in with a wooden spcon to make a smooth, soft icing.

10 Pour the icing evenly over the top of the cake, letting it run down the sides. Leave to set.

Chocolate hedgehog birthday cake

Ingredients
2 level tablespoons cocoa powder
2 tablespoons hot water
100g self-raising flour
1 level teaspoon baking powder
100g soft margarine
100g castor sugar
2 eggs
Icing
2 level tablespoons cocoa powder
2 tablespoons hot water
225g icing sugar
75g soft margarine
Decoration
50g blanched almonds
small sweets for the eyes, nose and mouth

Main cooking utensil
20-cm sandwich cake tin

Before you cook:
Arrange a shelf in the centre of the oven and heat the oven to moderate (170°C, 325°F, Gas Mark 3). Brush all round the inside of the tin with cooking oil and line the base with a circle of greaseproof paper; brush the paper with oil.

1 Put the cocoa powder in a basin, add the hot water and mix together with a tablespoon.
2 Place a sieve over a mixing bowl and sieve in the flour and baking powder. Add the soft margarine, sugar, eggs and blended cocoa powder. Stir all the ingredients together with a wooden spoon to make a smooth mixture.
3 Spoon into the cake tin and smooth the surface. Place in the oven and bake for 40 minutes.
4 Put on the oven gloves and take the cake out of the oven. Carefully turn it on to a wire tray and peel off the paper. Leave the cake to cool and switch off the oven.
5 To make the icing, mix the cocoa powder and hot water

together in a bowl. Sieve in the icing sugar, add the margarine
and with a wooden spoon mix all the ingredients together.

6 Cut the cake in half vertically, making two semi-circles. Sandwich the halves together with a little of the icing, and trim one end
to a point to make the nose. Place the cake on a flat board or plate
and spread the rest of the icing all over the cake. Smooth the nose
and face and make marks in the icing with the prongs of a fork all
over the body and going in the same direction.

7 Cut the almonds into strips and stick them all over the
hedgehog to represent his spikes. Stick jelly sweets in the icing for
his nose and eyes.

Shrove Tuesday pancakes

Shrove Tuesday is the last day before Lent. Pancakes were traditionally made and served on Shrove Tuesday to use up those ingredients which couldn't be eaten during Lent, as it is a time for fasting.

Makes 10-15 pancakes

Ingredients
100g plain flour
$\frac{1}{4}$ level teaspoon salt
2 eggs
300ml milk
cooking oil for frying
sugar and lemon wedges for serving

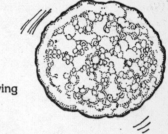

Main cooking utensil
non-stick frying pan

Before you cook:
Heat the oven to cool (130°C, 250°F, Gas Mark $\frac{1}{4}$) to keep the first batch of pancakes warm while you are cooking the rest. Have ready a dinner plate and a piece of foil to cover the pancakes.

1 Sieve the flour and salt into a mixing bowl. Make a well in the centre of the flour and break in the eggs.
2 With a wooden spoon, gradually mix the eggs into the flour. Still mixing with the wooden spoon, gradually pour in the milk. This mixture is called batter.
3 Beat the batter for 2 minutes to make sure that it is smooth and free from lumps, then pour it into a jug.
4 Put 2 teaspoons of oil in the frying pan and put it over a moderate heat.

5 Give the batter in the jug a stir and pour a little into the pan so that it makes a thin layer over the bottom. Cook for about 30 seconds until the underside is brown and the top is covered with little bubbles.

6 Toss or turn the pancake with a palette knife and cook the other side. Tip the pancake on to a plate, sprinkle with castor sugar and cover lightly with a piece of foil. Keep it warm in the oven while you are cooking the others, and as each one is cooked add it to the pile, sugar it and cover with foil.

7 When all the pancakes are cooked, turn off the heat and the oven. Take out the pancakes, roll each one up, place it on a plate and serve with wedges of lemon.

Here are two savoury recipes you may like to make for a birthday tea.

Tomato dip

Serves 6

Ingredients
225g pork chipolata sausages
4 tablespoons mayonnaise
1 tablespoon cream
2 tablespoons tomato purée
2-3 drops Worcestershire sauce

Main cooking utensil
grill pan

1 Place the sausages on the grill pan with the grill turned to moderate and cook for 15 minutes, turning them with kitchen tongs so that they brown evenly. Switch off the grill and place the sausages on a plate to cool.

2 To make the tomato dip, place the mayonnaise in a small basin and add the cream, tomato purée and Worcestershire sauce. Mix all the ingredients together with a tablespoon, then spoon the dip into a serving bowl standing on a large plate.

3 Cut each sausage into four pieces and into each piece push a cocktail stick. Pile the sausages around the bowl of tomato dip.

Cheesy pinwheels

Serves 4

Ingredients
150g cream cheese
50g soft butter
1 large unsliced white loaf
gherkins

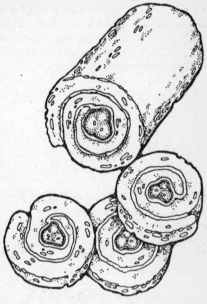

1 Place the cream cheese and butter in a basin and mix together with a wooden spoon.

2 Ask a grown-up to remove the crusts from the loaf and to cut the bread, lengthwise, into slices.

3 Spread each slice with some of the cheese mixture.

4 Place the gherkins on one narrow end of each slice of bread and roll it up like a mini Swiss roll.

5 Wrap each roll in cling film and chill in the refrigerator for 30 minutes.

6 Unwrap the rolls and place seam-side down on a board.

7 Cut each roll into 3 or 4 slices and arrange on a plate in a wheel shape.

Here are three recipes for Hallowe'en party food and one for a punch. In addition serve bowls of crisps, nuts and little savoury biscuits.

Bits on sticks

Take a whole grapefruit and stand it in a sundae dish. Collect a selection of the following ingredients: **canned pineapple cubes, cubes of Cheddar cheese, canned cocktail sausages, pickled onions, cocktail cherries** and thread three or four items on each cocktail stick. Press the cocktail sticks into the grapefruit. The grapefruit won't be wasted as it can be served for breakfast the following day.

Sausage parcels

Makes 8 parcels

Ingredients
8 rashers streaky bacon
8 skinless sausages

Main cooking utensil
grill pan

Before you cook:
Heat the grill to moderate.

1 With a pair of kitchen scissors, cut off the rinds from the bacon.
2 Wrap a rasher of bacon around each sausage. Place the sausage parcels on the grid of the grill pan and cook under the grill for 10 minutes, turning the sausages with a pair of tongs half-way through the cooking time so that they cook evenly.
3 Turn off the grill, remove the sausage parcels and insert a cocktail stick into each one. Lift on to a warmed plate for serving.

Chicken drumsticks with barbecue sauce

Serves 4

Ingredients
4 chicken drumsticks
cooking oil for brushing
salt and pepper
Sauce
1 small onion
425-g can tomatoes
1 tablespoon cooking oil
2 teaspoons Worcestershire sauce
few drops chilli sauce
pinch sugar

Main cooking utensil
grill pan

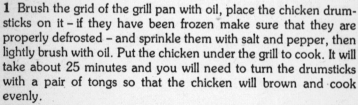

Before you cook:
Heat the grill to moderate.

1 Brush the grid of the grill pan with oil, place the chicken drumsticks on it – if they have been frozen make sure that they are properly defrosted – and sprinkle them with salt and pepper, then lightly brush with oil. Put the chicken under the grill to cook. It will take about 25 minutes and you will need to turn the drumsticks with a pair of tongs so that the chicken will brown and cook evenly.

2 To make the sauce, first peel and chop the onion. Open the can of tomatoes, place the oil in a pan and put over a moderate heat. Add the onion and cook for 2-3 minutes. To the pan add the tomatoes, Worcestershire sauce, chilli sauce and sugar.

3 Allow the sauce to come to the boil, then turn down the heat and let the sauce simmer for 10 minutes.

4 Turn off the grill and with a pair of tongs lift the chicken drumsticks on to a warmed serving plate. Serve the sauce separately in a jug.

Witches' brew

Makes enough for 6-7 tumblers

Ingredients
2 oranges
6 sugar lumps
300ml water
600ml canned pineapple juice
600ml apple juice
3 cloves
Decoration
1 apple
1 orange

Main cooking utensil
saucepan

1 Wash the two oranges and rub the sugar lumps over their skin so that they absorb the flavour. Place the sugar lumps in the pan. Cut the oranges in half and squeeze out the juice; pour the juice in the pan with the sugar lumps. Add the water.

2 Place the pan over a moderate heat until the sugar lumps dissolve, then pour in the pineapple and apple juices and add the cloves. Allow to heat through, but do not let the mixture boil.

3 Wash the apple and the other orange. Slice the orange; quarter, core and slice the apple.

4 Ask a grown-up to help you pour the hot punch into a large mixing bowl, then add the orange and apple slices.

5 Ladle the punch into warmed tumblers.

Perhaps the most special occasion of all is Christmas, when we have many traditional dishes. It is a very busy time for Mum, but you could help by making the mince pies. It is traditional to cut three slits in the top of each mince pie – one for each of the Three Wise men.

Mince pies

Makes 10-12 mince pies

Ingredients
200g plain flour
$\frac{1}{4}$ level teaspoon salt
100g margarine
2 tablespoons cold water
mincemeat
milk and sugar to glaze

Main cooking utensil
patty tins

Before you cook:
Arrange an oven shelf on the second runner and heat the oven to moderately hot (200°C, 400°F, Gas Mark 6).

1 Sieve the flour and salt into a mixing bowl. Add the margarine and rub it into the flour mixture with your fingertips until the mixture looks like breadcrumbs.
2 Add the water and with a table knife mix it in to form a dough. Gather the dough up with your hands and turn it on to a floured table.
3 Take two-thirds of the dough and roll it out thinly with a lightly floured rolling pin. Cut out rounds using a cutter (it can be fluted or plain) a little larger than the patty tins. Gather up the scraps and roll them out again to cut out more rounds.
4 Press a round into each patty tin, taking care not to stretch the pastry.
5 Put a well-filled teaspoon of mincemeat in each lined patty tin.
6 Take the remaining dough and roll it out thinly as before. Cut out circles for the tops of the pies, using a slightly smaller cutter.

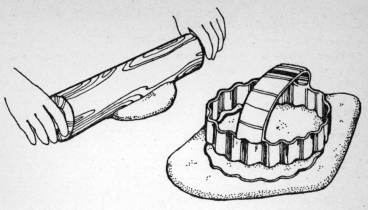

7 Brush the edges of the tops with water and place them on top of each mince pie, pressing the edges together to seal the mincemeat in.

8 Brush the tops with milk and sprinkle with castor sugar. Make the three slits and bake the mince pies for 20 minutes, until golden brown. Turn off the oven.

9 Remove the mince pies to a wire tray with a palette knife and leave to cool.

Bonfire Night on 5th November calls for hearty, warming food which can be eaten around the bonfire.

Sausage rolls make good bonfire fare. You can make them earlier in the day and just before you want to eat them, place them on a baking tray and re-heat in a slow oven. (150°C, 300°F, Gas Mark 2) for 10 minutes.

Sausage rolls

Makes 8 sausage rolls

Ingredients
378-g packet frozen puff pastry
200g pork sausage meat
milk to glaze

Main cooking utensil
baking tray

Before you cook:
Arrange an oven shelf on the second runner and heat the oven to hot (220°C, 425°F, Gas Mark 7). Allow the frozen puff pastry to thaw.

1 Lightly flour a part of the table top and with a rolling pin roll out the pastry until it makes a rectangle about 20 cm by 30 cm. With a knife cut the rectangle down the middle into two even-sized strips.
2 Lightly flour your hands and divide the sausage meat into two portions. Make each portion into a roll the length of each pastry strip.
3 Put a roll of sausage meat down the centre of each pastry strip and brush one long edge of each strip with a little milk.
4 Fold one side of the pastry over the sausage meat and with your fingers press the two pastry edges firmly together. Brush each roll with milk.
5 With a sharp knife cut each roll into four portions and make two or three slits on the top of each. Place on the baking tray and cook in the oven for 20 minutes.
6 Turn off the oven and remove the sausage rolls. Serve warm.

Harlequin soup

Serves 6

Ingredients
1 packet minestrone soup
900ml cold water
432-g can red kidney beans
2 frankfurters

Main cooking utensil
saucepan

1 Tip the contents from the packet of soup into the saucepan and add the cold water. Open the kidney beans and slice the frankfurters.
2 Place the pan over a moderate heat, and stirring with a wooden spoon, bring the mixture to the boil. Turn down the heat and add the kidney beans with the liquid from the can and the frankfurters.
3 Cover the pan with a lid and leave the soup to simmer for 15 minutes, then turn off the heat.
4 Ladle the soup into warmed mugs for serving.

Hot herb bread

Serves 6

Ingredients
100g butter
1 tablespoon chopped parsley
1 tablespoon chopped chives
½ level teaspoon dried mixed herbs
1 French loaf

Before you cook:
Heat the oven to moderately hot (200°C, 400°F, Gas Mark 6).

1 Put the butter in a basin and beat it with a wooden spoon until it is soft. Mix in the parsley, chives and mixed herbs.
2 With a sharp knife, slice the French loaf diagonally, but do not cut it right through.

3 Spread the herb butter on both sides of each slice with a small palette knife.
4 Wrap the loaf in a piece of foil and heat it in the oven for 15 minutes.
5 Turn off the oven, put on the oven gloves and take out the bread. Open the foil and break off and eat pieces of the delicious herb bread while it is still hot. It would go well with soup.

PART II OUTDOOR EATING

When the sun shines it is fun to pack up a picnic and go on an outing – to the park, the countryside or the seaside – or to pack up a knapsack and set off on a hike, a bike ride or even a pony ride. You may be planning a camping holiday, or simply want to put the tent up in the back garden and be self-sufficient for the day. The recipes in this section provide delicious food for all these occasions, and as well as having fun preparing the goodies you will have a wonderful time eating them, as food always tastes even better in the open air.

Planning the food for a picnic or expedition

For a family picnic, instead of making a mountain of boring sandwiches take French bread, baps or rolls with a selection of food to go with them. You could include, for example, hard-boiled eggs, cubes of cheese, slices of salami or other meats, savoury flan, cooked chicken portions or sausages. Wrap each item separately in foil and pack in an insulated box so that everything keeps cool on the journey.

You will also need to take some salad ingredients, such as tomatoes, spring onions or cucumber, or if you are ambitious, you may like to include some specially prepared salads – see the recipes on pages 119 and 121. Don't forget the butter, salt and pepper, cutlery and paper plates and napkins.

Remember to take cooling drinks. Either carry cans, or make up squashes and carry them in polythene tumblers in the insulated box. If you are especially fond of tea or coffee, or if the weather is not very warm, take some boiling water in a vacuum flask so that you can make your own hot drinks with teabags and instant coffee. Don't forget the sugar and milk – dried milk is best to take on a picnic.

To round off the meal, take some sort of cake or biscuits, yogurts if you like them, and fresh fruit. Apples, oranges and bananas are best as they won't get squashed if you pack them carefully.

Finally, an important point, remember to collect all your litter after the picnic, and if there is no litter bin handy, take it back home to put in the dustbin. Other people may want to use your picnic spot and they won't enjoy sitting in the middle of your discarded rubbish!

Instead of a picnic, you may be planning an expedition – a hike, bike ride or pony ride. If so, you will want to take some food with you to keep you going. Remember that you will have to carry the food in a knapsack along with your map and maybe small books on birds, trees or flowers so you can't take anything too heavy or too awkward to pack. Remember, too, the golden rule of the countryside – bring your litter home with you.

On the following pages are some picnic ideas which you can make at home. The banana bars and teabread can be made 2-3 days before the picnic and stored in an airtight tin. Make the cheese loaf and the flan the day before as they do not keep so well.

Picnic flan

Serves 4

Ingredients
175g plain flour
75g margarine
1½ tablespoons water
Filling
75g Cheddar cheese
2 eggs
150ml milk
salt and pepper
1 tablespoon snipped chives

Main cooking utensil
18-cm foil baking case

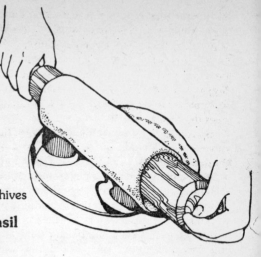

Before you cook:
Arrange a shelf on the second runner from the top and heat the oven to moderate (180°C, 350°F, Gas Mark 4).

1 Sieve the flour into a mixing bowl. Add the margarine and rub it into the flour until the mixture looks like breadcrumbs.
2 Add the water and mix it in with a knife, then using your hands form the mixture into a pastry dough.

118

3 Lightly flour part of the table and roll out the dough to form a circle a bit bigger than your foil case. Lift the circle of pastry on to the rolling pin and carefully lower it into the foil case to make a lining, pressing it down well with your fingers. Make the top edge neat by pinching the pastry all round with your thumb and first finger. Stand the foil dish on a baking tray.

4 Grate the cheese on to a piece of kitchen paper and sprinkle it over the pastry base.

5 Break the eggs into a basin and add the milk, salt and pepper, mixing these ingredients together with a fork. Now carefully pour them over the cheese and sprinkle the snipped chives on top.

6 Put the flan in the oven and bake for 30-35 minutes, until the filling is set.

7 Put on the oven gloves and take out the flan. Turn off the oven.

8 Leave to cool, then store in the refrigerator overnight.

For the picnic Cover the surface of the flan with a piece of foil and carry it in the insulated box, being careful not to pack anything on top of it.

Nutty cheese salad

Serves 4

Ingredients
1 lettuce
25g sultanas
100g Cheddar cheese
50g walnuts

1 Wash the lettuce in cold water and throw away any coarse leaves. Drain, and pat dry with kitchen paper.

2 Tear the lettuce leaves into small pieces with your fingers and place them in the bottom of a polythene container.

3 Cut the cheese into cubes and chop the walnuts.

4 Toss the cheese, walnuts and sultanas with the lettuce in the polythene container.

5 Leave in the refrigerator until you are ready to go on the picnic, then put the lid on the container and pack it in the insulated box.

Cheese loaf

This can be sliced and spread with butter, and is delicious eaten with cubes of cheese, cold meats and tomatoes.

Ingredients
75g Cheddar cheese
225g self-raising flour*
1 level teaspoon baking powder
1 level teaspoon dry mustard
½ level teaspoon salt
¼ level teaspoon pepper
75g soft margarine
1 egg
150ml cold milk

Main cooking utensil
450-g loaf tin

Before you cook:
Arrange a shelf in the centre of the oven and heat the oven to moderately hot (190°C, 375°F, Gas Mark 5). Brush all round the inside of the loaf tin with cooking oil and line the bottom with a piece of greaseproof paper, also brushed with oil.

1 Grate the cheese finely on to a piece of kitchen paper.
2 Place a sieve over a mixing bowl and sieve in the flour, baking powder, mustard, salt and pepper. Add the soft margarine, egg, cheese and milk.
3 Take a wooden spoon and stir all the ingredients together for 3-4 minutes, until well mixed.
4 Spoon the mixture into the tin and smooth the surface. Place in the oven and bake for 40-45 minutes, until firm and golden brown.
5 Put on the oven gloves, take out the loaf and turn off the oven.
6 Leave the loaf in the tin for 5 minutes, then with the oven gloves on turn it out on to a wire tray to cool.

*You can, if you like, make a cheese and onion loaf by substituting 25g of dried onion for 25g of the flour

For the picnic Cut the loaf into slices and spread each slice with butter. Put the loaf back together again, wrap it in foil and pack it in the insulated box to keep the butter fresh on the journey.

Hawaiian rice salad

Serves 4

Ingredients
225g long-grain rice
225-g can pineapple pieces
$\frac{1}{2}$ cucumber
1 green pepper
4 tablespoons mayonnaise

1 Half fill a large pan with water and add 1 level teaspoon salt. Put over a moderate heat and bring to the boil. Add the rice, lower the heat, cover the pan and cook for 5 minutes.

2 Drain the rice in a sieve (beware of the steam) and put it under cold running water to cool it and separate the grains. Drain well.

3 Open the can of pineapple. Drain off the juice into a jug and keep it. Wash and cube the cucumber. Wash the pepper, cut it in half, take out the seeds and cut the green part into cubes.

4 Put the mayonnaise in a basin and mix it with 2 tablespoons of the pineapple juice.

5 Place the rice, cucumber, green pepper cubes and pineapple pieces in a mixing bowl. Add the mayonnaise mixture and using a tablespoon, mix all the ingredients together.

For the picnic Spoon the salad into a polythene container, put on the lid and pack in the insulated box.

Banana bars

Makes 16 banana bars

Ingredients
175g plain chocolate
3 small bananas
50g margarine
100g castor sugar
4 tablespoons milk
1 egg
50g All-Bran
175g self-raising flour
1 level teaspoon salt
½ level teaspoon cinnamon

Main cooking utensil
18- by 23-cm Swiss roll tin

Before you cook:
Arrange a shelf in the centre of the oven and heat the oven to
moderate (180°C, 350°F, Gas Mark 4). Brush all round the inside
of the tin with cooking oil and line the base and sides with a piece
of greaseproof paper. Brush the paper with oil.

1 Break the chocolate into a basin. Put a saucepan half-filled with
water on to heat and stand the basin of chocolate over the pan.
Leave the chocolate to melt, stirring it with a wooden spoon from
time to time.
2 Peel the bananas, place them in another basin and mash with a
fork.
3 Put the margarine and sugar in a mixing bowl and beat them
together with a wooden spoon until light in colour and of a soft
consistency.
4 Add the mashed bananas, the milk and egg, and mix all these
ingredients together with the wooden spoon.
5 Turn off the heat under the pan and add the melted
chocolate – scraping the bowl out well – and the All-Bran to the
banana mixture.
6 Sieve the flour, salt and cinnamon into the mixing bowl and
mix everything together.

7 Spoon the mixture into the tin and smooth the surface. Put it in the oven and bake for 30-35 minutes, until firm.

8 Put on the oven gloves and take out the cake. Turn off the oven. Turn the cake out on to a wire tray and peel off the paper. Leave to cool.

9 When cool, put the cake on a board and cut it into 16 bars. Store them in an airtight tin.

For the picnic Wrap the bars in foil or pack them in a polythene box.

Delicious teabread

Ingredients
100g margarine
300ml tea without milk
175g mixed dried fruit
100g castor sugar
250g self-raising flour
1 level teaspoon bicarbonate of soda
$\frac{1}{4}$ level teaspoon salt

Main cooking utensil
900-g loaf tin

Before you cook:
Arrange a shelf in the centre of the oven and heat the oven to moderate (180°C, 350°F, Gas Mark 4). Brush all round the inside of the tin with cooking oil. Line the bottom of the tin with a piece of greaseproof paper, and brush that, too, with oil.

1 Put the margarine, tea, fruit and sugar in a pan over a low heat. Bring the mixture to the boil and let it simmer for 4 minutes. Turn off the heat and leave the mixture to cool.

2 Sieve the flour, bicarbonate of soda and salt into a mixing bowl.

3 Add the cooled mixture and with a wooden spoon mix all the ingredients together.

4 Spoon the mixture into the tin and smooth the surface. Put it in the oven and bake for 1-1$\frac{1}{4}$ hours.

5 Put on the oven gloves and take out the teabread. Turn off the oven.

6 Leave the loaf in the tin for 10 minutes, then turn it out on to a wire tray to cool.

7 Store in an airtight tin.

For the picnic Cut as many slices as you need and spread each one with butter. Put the slices together in pairs, buttered sides together, and wrap in foil. Carry in the insulated box.

The following three recipes are particularly suitable for carrying on an expedition; the lemonade is good any time!

Expedition sandwiches

Spread slices of brown or white bread with butter and make sandwiches using any of these tasty fillings:

1 Grated cheese mixed with chopped dates.
2 Hard-boiled egg mashed with sandwich spread.
3 Peanut butter.
4 Marmite and cress.
5 Bananas, peeled and mashed with chopped nuts.

124

Wrap the sandwiches in foil and then put them in a polythene box so that they won't get squashed. Also take an apple, and so that you don't die of thirst, some homemade lemonade, which you can carry in a polythene tumbler with a lid. You may also like to take some flapjacks, as they are not fragile, or slices of cheesy bacon scone and a few boiled sweets to suck.

Flapjacks

Makes 16 flapjacks

Ingredients
50g margarine
100g golden syrup
50g castor sugar
225g rolled oats

Main cooking utensil
18- by 23-cm Swiss roll tin

Before you cook:
Arrange a shelf in the centre of the oven and heat the oven to moderate (180°C, 350°F, Gas Mark 4). Brush the inside of the tin with cooking oil.

1 Place the margarine, syrup and castor sugar in a saucepan. Put over a moderate heat and stir with a wooden spoon until the ingredients have melted.
2 Remove the pan and turn off the heat. Add the rolled oats to the melted ingredients and stir them in with the wooden spoon.
3 Spread the mixture evenly in the tin, place in the oven and bake for 30-35 minutes.
4 Put on the oven gloves, take the tin out of the oven and turn off the oven.
5 Cut the mixture into 16 pieces and leave to cool in the tin.

For an expedition Wrap the pieces in foil.

Cheesy bacon scone

Test Cook Jessica especially enjoyed making this recipe in the
Hamlyn Kitchen.

Ingredients
3 rashers streaky bacon
50g Cheddar cheese
225g plain flour
2 level teaspoons baking powder
$\frac{1}{4}$ level teaspoon salt
$\frac{1}{4}$ level teaspoon dry mustard
50g margarine
150ml milk
1 tablespoon milk for glazing

Main cooking utensil
20-cm sandwich cake tin

Before you cook:
Arrange a shelf on the second runner of the oven and heat the
oven to hot (220°C, 425°F, Gas Mark 7). Brush the inside of the
sandwich cake tin with cooking oil.

1 Using kitchen scissors, remove the rinds from the bacon
rashers, then snip the rashers into small pieces.
2 Put the bacon in a frying pan over a moderate heat. Cook it for
3 minutes, stirring with a wooden spoon from time to time so that
all the pieces cook evenly.
3 Remove the pan and turn off the heat. Lift the bacon out on to
the kitchen paper placed on a small plate and put it aside until
later.
4 Grate the cheese on to a piece of kitchen paper. Sieve the
flour, baking powder, salt and mustard into a mixing bowl.
6 Add the margarine, and with your fingertips rub it into the flour
to make a mixture like breadcrumbs. Using a knife, stir in the
bacon and grated cheese. Add the milk and mix well.
7 Making sure the table is clean, sprinkle a little flour over a small
area. Lift the mixture on to the floured surface, knead it lightly
then roll it out to a round shape big enough to fit the tin.

8 Lift the rolled mixture into the tin and press it out to the edges. Brush the surface of the scone with the milk and place in the oven. Bake for 20 minutes.

9 Put on the oven gloves, remove the tin and turn off the oven.

10 Invert the tin over the wire tray to let the scone fall out, then turn it the right way up and leave it to cool.

For an expedition Cut the scone into wedges; halve each piece and spread with butter. Sandwich the two pieces together and wrap in foil.

Home-made lemonade

Makes enough for about 6 tumblers

Ingredients
3 lemons
2 tablespoons castor sugar
1·25 litres water
lemon slices
sprigs of mint

Main cooking utensil
saucepan

1 Wash and dry the lemons. With a sharp knife cut them into cubes and place them in a large heatproof jug or mixing bowl. Add the sugar.

2 Put the water in the saucepan and bring to the boil over a moderate heat. Pour the boiling water over the lemons and sugar, and leave for 20 minutes.

3 Pour the lemonade through a sieve into a clean jug and leave to chill in the refrigerator.

For an expedition Pour the lemonade into a polythene tumbler and add some lemon slices and sprigs of mint. Put on the lid, making sure it is secure.

Cooking for campers

It's great fun to go on a camping holiday and cook your own meals in your own way. If you *are* cooking outside, place the camping stove on a flat piece of ground, not too near the tent, but out of the wind. Be very careful when lighting it – it is best if a grown-up is around to help. Put a table or an upturned box next to the stove and a large bag to collect all the rubbish.

Food for hungry campers needs to be nourishing yet quick and simple to prepare, so here's a selection of recipes for you to try next time you go camping.

Tomato and cheese soup

Serves 4

Ingredients
425-g can tomatoes
3 sticks celery
600ml (about 2 large mugsful) water
1 chicken stock cube
salt and pepper
100g Cheddar cheese (about 10 x 7 x 3cm)

Main cooking utensil
saucepan

1 Open the can of tomatoes and tip the contents into the pan.
2 Cut the celery into small pieces and add to the tomatoes. Add the water, stock cube and a sprinkling of salt and pepper.
3 Place the pan on the camping stove and bring the soup to the boil, then cover the pan with a lid and leave it to simmer for 30 minutes.
4 Cut the cheese into cubes and stir into the soup. Turn off the heat.
5 Ladle the soup into bowls and serve with bread rolls or pieces of French bread.

Cheese snack

Serves 2

Ingredients
4 slices bread
100g butter
2 slices cheese
2 slices ham

Main cooking utensil
frying pan

1 Cut the crusts off the bread and spread each slice with some of the butter.

2 On two of the bread slices place a slice each of cheese and ham. Top with the remaining bread slices to make a sandwich.
3 Place the remaining butter in the frying pan and melt over the camping stove. Add the sandwiches and fry them on one side for 4 minutes, then turn them over with a fish slice and fry for another 4 minutes on the other side. Turn off the heat and serve.

Ranch house stew

Serves 4

Ingredients
1 onion
2 carrots
425-g can stewed steak
1 tablespoon cooking oil
1 beef stock cube
900ml (about 3 large mugsful) water
15 level tablespoons long-grain rice
salt and pepper

Main cooking utensil
saucepan

1 Peel and chop the onion; scrape and slice the carrots, and open the can of stewed steak.

2 Pour the oil into the pan, heat it over the camping stove, then add the onion and carrots and cook for 4 minutes.

3 Add the stewed steak, crumbled stock cube, water, rice, salt and pepper. Bring the mixture to the boil, stirring meanwhile, then lower the heat, cover and simmer for 15 minutes.

Corned beef hash

Serves 4

Ingredients
1 onion
340-g can corned beef
220-g can baked beans
400-g can potatoes
1 tablespoon cooking oil
salt and pepper

Main cooking utensil
saucepan

1 Peel and chop the onion. Open the cans of corned beef and baked beans; open and drain the can of potatoes.

2 Pour the oil into the pan and heat over the camping stove. Add the onion and cook until it has softened.

3 Cut the corned beef into cubes and add to the pan together with the potatoes, baked beans and a sprinkling of salt and pepper.

4 Cook over the heat, stirring the hash with a wooden spoon until it is piping hot. Turn off the heat and serve.

Mexican mince

Serves 4

Ingredients
425-g can minced beef
141-g can baked beans
432-g can tomato soup
$\frac{1}{4}$ soup can water
2 level teaspoons chilli powder

Main cooking utensil
saucepan

1 Open the cans of minced beef, baked beans and tomato soup.
2 Tip the minced beef into a pan and heat it on the camping stove, stirring with a wooden spoon.
3 Add the tomato soup, water and chilli powder. Stir the ingredients together, let them come to the boil then cover and simmer for 15 minutes.
4 Stir in the baked beans and cook for a further 5 minutes. Turn off the heat.
5 Serve with rolls or bread.

Sausage quickie

Serves 4

Ingredients
1 onion
1 tablespoon cooking oil
225g pork sausages
425-g can mushroom soup
$\frac{1}{2}$ the soup can of water
198-g can sweetcorn

Main cooking utensil
saucepan

1 Peel and slice the onion. Pour the oil into the pan, heat it on the camping stove, then add the onion and sausages and cook until browned. Tip out any extra fat.
2 Add the mushroom soup, together with half the can full of water. Bring to the boil, then lower the heat, cover and simmer for 15 minutes.
3 Open the can of sweetcorn, add to the pan and simmer for a further 5 minutes. Turn off the heat.
4 Serve with bread.

Candied bananas

Serves 4

Ingredients
4 bananas
75g butter
3 level tablespoons brown sugar

Main cooking utensil
frying pan

1 Peel the bananas and cut each one in half lengthways.
2 Put the butter in the pan and melt it over the camping stove. Add the bananas and turn them with a palette knife so that they are coated with butter.
3 Now sprinkle in the sugar and cook until it melts. Turn off the heat.
4 Lift the bananas on to a plate and pour over the delicious caramel.

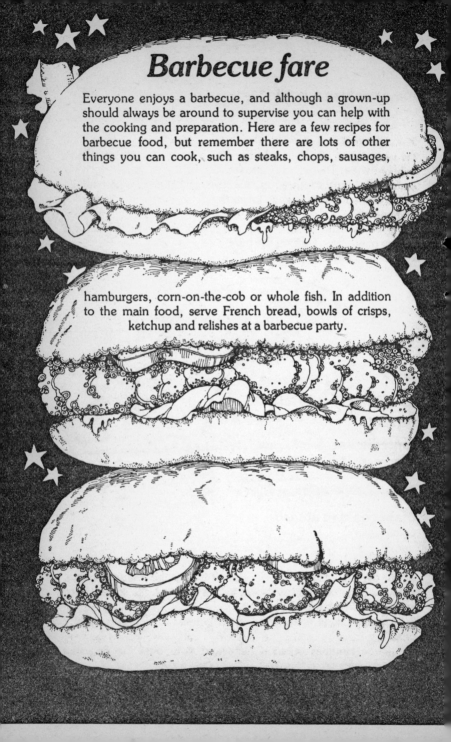

Barbecue fare

Everyone enjoys a barbecue, and although a grown-up should always be around to supervise you can help with the cooking and preparation. Here are a few recipes for barbecue food, but remember there are lots of other things you can cook, such as steaks, chops, sausages, hamburgers, corn-on-the-cob or whole fish. In addition to the main food, serve French bread, bowls of crisps, ketchup and relishes at a barbecue party.

Barbecued chicken

Serves 4

Ingredients
4 chicken joints
4 sprigs fresh rosemary
2 tablespoons lemon juice
3 tablespoons cooking oil
1 tablespoon Worcestershire sauce
few drops Tabasco sauce
1 clove garlic
4 teaspoons tomato ketchup·

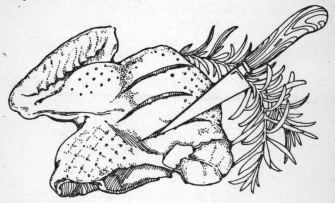

1 With a sharp-pointed knife make deep cuts into the flesh of the chicken. Put the joints in the bottom of a shallow dish and add the rosemary sprigs.

2 In a small bowl mix together the lemon juice, oil, Worcestershire sauce, Tabasco sauce, peeled garlic clove and tomato ketchup.

3 Pour this mixture over the chicken joints and leave in the refrigerator to marinate, or soak, for several hours.

4 Later, when the barbecue is hot, take the chicken joints out of the marinade mixture and place them on the rack over the coals. Cook for 10 minutes on one side, then with a pair of tongs turn the joints over and cook for another 10 minutes. During the cooking brush the chicken with some of the marinade.

Sausage and pineapple kebabs

Serves 4

Ingredients
8 chipolata sausages
8 rashers streaky bacon
340-g can pineapple chunks
cooking oil for brushing
4 small packets potato crisps

1 Hold each sausage by its ends and twist so that it almost breaks in the middle. Snip each sausage in half with a pair of kitchen scissors, making 16 small sausages.
2 Cut the rinds off the bacon rashers and cut each rasher in two.
3 Open the can of pineapple chunks and drain off the juice. (You can drink this.) Wrap each piece of pineapple in a bacon rasher half.
4 Take four kebab skewers and on to each skewer thread, alternately, a sausage and a bacon-wrapped piece of pineapple.

5 Lay the kebabs over the barbecue and brush them with oil. Cook for 10 minutes, turning them so that they brown evenly.
6 Serve with the potato crisps.

Skewered sausage balls

Serves 4

Ingredients
450g pork sausagemeat
2 level tablespoons sage and onion stuffing mix
8 button mushrooms
4 bay leaves
cooking oil for brushing
Barbecue sauce
425-g can tomatoes
1 tablespoon tomato purée
1 tablespoon Worcestershire sauce
2 teaspoons French mustard

1 In a bowl mix together the sausagemeat and stuffing mix. With your hands, form the mixture into 12 even-sized balls. Wipe the mushrooms with a piece of damp kitchen paper.
2 Take four skewers and on to each one thread three sausage balls, two mushrooms and one bay leaf.
3 Place over the barbecue, brush with oil and cook for 15-20 minutes, turning the skewers so that the food browns evenly.
4 While the kebabs are cooking, open the can of tomatoes and tip them into a saucepan. Add the tomato purée, Worcestershire sauce and French mustard, and place on the grid of the barbecue to heat. Serve the sauce with the kebabs.

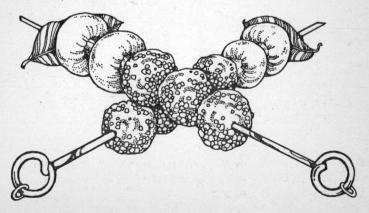

Index